BOY SCOUTS OF AMERICA
MERIT BADGE SERIES

GOLF

BOY SCOUTS OF AMERICA®

Requirements

1. Discuss safety on the golf course. Show that you know first aid for injuries or illnesses that could occur while golfing, including heat reactions, dehydration, blisters, sprains, and strains.

2. Study the USGA "Rules of Golf" now in use.
    a. Tell about the three categories of golf etiquette.
    b. Demonstrate that you understand the definitions of golf terms.
    c. Show that you understand the "Rules of Amateur Status."

3. Tell about your understanding of the USGA system of handicapping.

4. Do the following:
    a. Tell about the early history of golf.
    b. Describe golf's early years in the United States.
    c. Tell about the accomplishments of a top golfer of your choice.

5. Discuss with your counselor vocational opportunities related to golf.

6. Do the following:
    a. Tell how golf can contribute to a healthy lifestyle, mentally and physically.
    b. Tell how a golf exercise plan can help you play better. Show two exercises that would help improve your game.

7. Show the following:

    a. The proper grip, stance, posture, and key fundamentals of a good swing

    b. The full wood shot, played from a tee

    c. The fairway wood shot

    d. The long iron shot

    e. The short iron shot

    f. The approach, chip-and-run, and pitch shots

    g. The sand iron shot, bunker, or heavy rough recovery shots

    h. A sound putting stroke

8. Play a minimum of two nine-hole rounds or one 18-hole round of golf with another golfer about your age and with your counselor, or an adult approved by your counselor. Do the following:

    a. Follow the "Rules of Golf."

    b. Practice good golf etiquette.

    c. Show respect to fellow golfers, committee, sponsor, and gallery.

Contents

Introduction 7
Golf Lingo 16
Tools of the Game 23
How to Play the Game 29
Safety, First Aid, and Fitness 52
Conduct and Procedures on the Golf Course 59
Major Influences 65
Careers in Golf 73
Golf Resources 77

Introduction

Golf is an outdoor game played on a course that includes greens, fairways, roughs, and usually bunkers and water hazards. A standard round of golf includes playing 18 holes over a course that measures about 6,000 to 8,000 yards. Each hole

- Includes a tee area, fairway, rough, and green, and usually varies in length from 100 to 600 yards
- Begins from a teeing ground and ends at a green that has a cup that is 4.5 inches in diameter, dug into the green and marked with a flagstick
- Has a "par" (predetermined number of strokes to complete play)

The object of golf is to get the golf ball, using specially designed golf clubs, into the cup (also known as the hole) in as few strokes as possible, following the "Rules of Golf." Players try to drive the ball from the teeing ground (the starting point) to the fairway to the green, which has closely cut grass. Usually on each side of the fairway is the rough, which can include long grass, trees, and bushes. Fairway bunkers and water hazards can provide other obstacles. Once a player reaches the green, he uses a putter to roll the ball over the surface of the green and into the hole.

Each hole on a course is rated as a par 3, par 4, or par 5, depending on its length. For example, a hole is determined to be a par 3 if a golfer is able to reach the green in one shot from the tee. Two putts is considered the standard for each hole, so by reaching the green on a par 3 in one shot and two-putting, a golfer is said to have "parred" the hole. It should take two shots to reach a par 4 and three to reach a par 5. Par for an 18-hole course is determined by adding the total par scores for all 18 holes.

The two most common forms of play in golf are stroke play (also called medal play) and match play. In stroke play, a player counts each swing attempted at the ball and adds them for the total score. In competition, the player with the fewest

Introduction

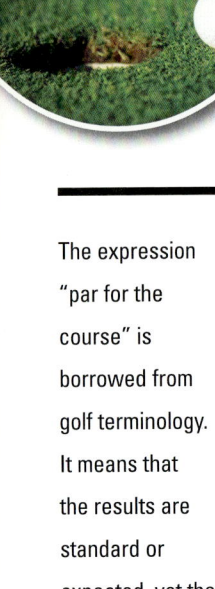

strokes over a set number of holes is the winner. Ties usually are decided by playoffs, or extra holes. When two or more players remain tied after completing a playoff of a predetermined number of holes, those golfers enter a *sudden-death* playoff in which the first to win a hole is declared the winner. There also can be stroke play among teams, with the lowest team score winning.

Match play can be individual against individual or team against team. The individual or team taking the fewest strokes on a hole wins that hole. The individual or team that wins the most holes wins the match. If a hole is tied in number of strokes, that hole is said to be "halved." A match that ends *all square* (in a tie) usually is decided by a playoff, with the winner being the first to win a hole.

> In match play, a match has gone *dormie* when a player or team leads the opponent by the same number of holes still to play. (For example, a player leads by four holes with four holes remaining.) If the lead player wins one more hole, then the competition is over. If, however, the opponent wins all the remaining holes, then the score would be "all square" and the winner is determined by a hole-by-hole playoff.

Golf is unique because the players police themselves. Other sports depend upon referees or umpires to apply penalties when there are infractions of the rules. Golf also has officials, but seldom are there enough to watch every player in a tournament. So, it is up to individual players and their opponents to call a penalty if a rule is violated. Every player is expected to act honorably, and the welfare and integrity of the game rely on every player's honesty. This is why golf often is referred to as a "gentleman's game."

Early History

Artifacts, drawings, and writings indicate that humans have been hitting an object with a stick for hundreds, if not thousands, of years. Out of these primitive beginnings, the game has evolved into the vastly popular worldwide sport it is today.

Most historians believe that games using a stick to hit an object, often a stone or feather-filled bag, were played at least as far back as Roman times and probably earlier. The Romans called their game "paganica."

The expression "par for the course" is borrowed from golf terminology. It means that the results are standard or expected, yet the speaker's feelings are negative—as in this example: *My teacher said we have to make up the snow day on Saturday. Well, that's par for the course.*

INTRODUCTION

In the 17th century, the Dutch played a game called "colve" or "kolven." Some historians have said that the word "golf" originated from "kolven," but others believe the word and game of golf originated from "gowf,"' or "golfe," a game played by the Scots over pastures and fields.

Golf's origin might always be debated, but most experts agree that the game that most resembles what is played today originated in Scotland in the 14th or 15th century. The game caught on and became so popular with the common people in Scotland that the Scottish Parliament passed laws three times in the 15th century prohibiting people from playing golf. (The government wanted to develop more proficient archers, who could be used for military purposes.) However, most Scots ignored the laws and continued to golf. Scotland's King James IV began playing the game in the 16th century, and golf soon became a game favored by royalty and the rich.

One of the first premier golf courses was Leith, near Glasgow. The first club to form an annual competition was the Gentlemen Golfers of Leith, which began in 1744 and was later renamed the Honourable Company of Edinburgh Golfers. The St. Andrews Society of Golfers was established in 1754 and also began annual competitions, using Leith's rules. The first golf club formed outside Scotland was the Royal Blackheath, near London, in 1766, though there are indications that the game had been played there for more than 100 years.

> Numerous golfers have had to call a penalty on themselves, sometimes in major tournaments. The golfer often does not realize he or she has violated a rule. It is important to know the rules.

> One of the first famous women to play was Mary, Queen of Scots. She began playing in France, and the young men who attended her were cadets, or students. The term later became "caddy," or "caddie" in Scotland and England, and that term is still used today for those who carry the golf bags for golfers.

Golf also became competitive. The first major championship was the British Open in 1860 in Prestwick, Scotland. There were only eight competitors, and Willie Park won the first title. Stroke play had been introduced in 1759, and six years later, the first 18-hole course, which became the standard, was constructed at St. Andrews, Scotland.

Golf eventually was introduced to India, France, Canada, Hong Kong, and the United States. Evidence suggests that golf was being played in New York in 1779. The growth of the rail system in the United States resulted in more golf courses being built.

> By 1900, there were more than 1,000 golf courses in the United States.

Introduction

A view of the Old Course at St. Andrews in Scotland

A *links* course is normally built along a coastal area. Because of the sandy soil and constant wind, the course features dunes, very deep sand bunkers called pot bunkers, and very few—if any—trees.

The United States Golf Association was established in 1894 and, besides publishing rules of the game, it established a handicapping system, began conducting major amateur and open tournaments, and began funding turf and grass research, among other things.

In 1895, the USGA began the U.S. Open and the U.S. Ladies Amateur tournaments, and in 1911, John McDermott became the first American-born player to win the U.S. Open. Two years later, interest in golf blossomed even more when 20-year-old Francis Ouimet, an American amateur, won the U.S. Open by beating Englishmen Harry Vardon and Ted Ray, two of the world's best players, in a playoff. It was an astonishing upset because Ouimet, a former caddie, was a virtual unknown.

Ouimet's victory was considered a turning point for American golf because, until then, golf had been dominated by players from England and Scotland. There were few players in the United States, and the game was played at golf clubs, mostly by the wealthy. Within 10 years of Ouimet's victory, the number of golfers in the United States was said to have tripled and more courses—including public courses—were built.

Modern Golf

In the United States, the Professional Golf Association of America was established in 1916 when a group of New York–area professionals and amateurs met at a meeting hosted by businessman Rodman Wanamaker in an effort to organize their sport. By 1944, the PGA had formed a nationwide tour of 22 events. In 1968, a players' organization broke away from the PGA, but eventually it compromised and formed the Tournament Players Division of PGA. That organization is now known as the PGA Tour.

INTRODUCTION

In 1927, the Ryder Cup matches began with American golfers competing against the British and Irish. Early on, the Americans dominated the biennial match play event. Only since 1979, when golfers outside the British Isles were allowed to be on the European team, has the Ryder Cup become more competitive. But it was not until 1985 that the Europeans ended a 28-year U.S. victory streak. Since then, the Ryder Cup has grown into an intense rivalry.

One of the first U.S. golfers to gain nationwide and worldwide notoriety was Robert Tyre "Bobby" Jones Jr., who won 13 national championships and the original "grand slam"—the U.S. and British Amateurs, and the U.S. and British Opens—in 1930.

Jones teamed with Clifford Roberts and began building Augusta National Golf Club in 1930 in Augusta, Georgia. They began the Augusta National Invitation Tournament for a select list of players in 1934. The tournament's name soon was changed to the Masters, and it has since become one of the four major tournaments in the world, along with the U.S. and British Opens and the PGA Championship.

Great women golfers of the time were Joyce Wethered, who won five consecutive English Ladies Championship titles, and Glenna Collett Vare, who won six U.S. Women Amateur titles. The first women's U.S. Open was in 1946, and the Ladies Professional Golf Association was formed in 1951.

World War II interrupted most international play in the early 1940s, but interest in the game revived after the inspirational comeback of Ben Hogan (who nearly died in 1949 when his car collided with a bus) and the beginning of television coverage in the 1950s. Other popular male golfers of that time included Gene Sarazen, Walter Hagen, Tommy Armour, and Byron Nelson.

Another major step came in 1961 when the PGA eliminated its "whites only" rule, and Charlie Sifford became the first African American to play the tour. In 1975, Lee Elder became the first African American to compete in the Masters.

> An *open* tournament is an event in which both professional and amateur golfers are eligible to compete.

While African Americans have excelled in almost every professional sport, their success in golf has been slower. One factor is because the PGA did not allow African American golfers to compete on the tour until 1961. Economics and social barriers also contributed because for many years the sport was played mainly at country clubs with whites-only membership. Over the years, one of the game's most positive advancements has been the elimination of such barriers.

Introduction

Most golf historians credit the charismatic Arnold Palmer, with his go-for-broke play and memorable comebacks, and golfing President Dwight Eisenhower with further spurring the golf craze. In the 1960s, Palmer, powerful Jack Nicklaus, and South African Gary Player became known as the Big Three because of their constant success, especially in major tournaments.

> The U.S. Amateur and British Amateur tournaments are no longer part of the grand slam. To win today's grand slam, a professional golfer must win each of the four major tournaments—the Masters, PGA Championship, U.S. Open, and British Open—in one calendar year. No one has ever won the modern grand slam, but Gene Sarazen, Ben Hogan, Gary Player, Jack Nicklaus, and Tiger Woods have won career grand slams, which means they have won each of the major tournaments at least once.

Nicklaus won a record 26 major titles, including two U.S. Amateur Championships and six Senior PGA Championships. Many experts believed Nicklaus' record would never be challenged because of the increased competition worldwide. However, the emergence of Tiger Woods in the 1990s changed those attitudes. By his early 20s, Woods already had won 10 major titles—four of them consecutive.

Meanwhile, golf has continued to attract more juniors, women, and minorities; professionals are playing for millions of dollars; and equipment continues to evolve to help make striking a ball easier for the average player. Golf is still a staple of sports media coverage.

The National Golf Foundation reported in 2007 that there were 28.7 million golfers, 17 percent of whom are juniors 6 to 17 years old. By 2007, the number of golf courses in the United States was approximately 16,000.

Governing Bodies

The organizations that establish the golf rules for most of the world are the Royal and Ancient Golf Club of St. Andrews and the United States Golf Association. Members of these organizations meet and communicate continually to review, improve, clarify, and amend the rules to assure uniformity, and both bodies must agree before changes are enacted.

INTRODUCTION

The professional golf organizations in the United States are the PGA of America, the Ladies Professional Golf Association, the PGA Tour (which includes senior and secondary tours), and the LPGA Tour. Members of the PGA include club, public, and teaching professionals. The professional tours include men and women who mainly compete for a living. Similar golf organizations have been formed in all parts of the world.

Changes in Equipment

Golf equipment has changed drastically over the years, from clubs made from a single piece of wood to the high-tech wonders of today. The first golf balls also were quite primitive, being made of wood.

The first big change in golf balls was when the "feathery" was introduced in the 17th century. These usually were handmade stitched horsehide stuffed with compressed feathers. The maximum distance these balls could be driven was about 175 yards. During the 19th century, featheries were replaced by the gutta-percha ball, which was made from the latex of tropical trees, and the driving distance increased to almost 200 yards.

The "feathery," circa early 1700

In 1898, the B. F. Goodrich Company and Coburn Haskell of Akron, Ohio, introduced a ball with a solid rubber core wrapped in rubber strips. This evolved to the production of balls with liquid cores and various covers with dimples, and has led to the modern-day golf ball. Golf balls now must have a diameter of no less than 1.68 inches and weigh not more than 1.62 ounces to be legal, according to the rules of the sport's governing bodies.

As equipment evolved, clubheads in Scotland and England were made of different woods, usually from beech or fruit trees. The shafts also were wooden, usually made from ash or hazel, and makers of the clubs were considered skilled craftsmen.

The modern-day golf ball

In the 1800s, persimmon was the main wood used for clubheads, and hickory for the shafts. The grips usually were leather and quite slick. Hand-forged irons were introduced in the 19th century. Most clubs were known by names, such as spoon, mashie, and niblick, not numbers. In the 1930s, steel shafts began replacing the wooden ones, causing players to adjust their swings to take advantage of the more consistent and stronger shafts.

GOLF

INTRODUCTION

Modern-day clubs include more high-tech materials such as titanium, graphite, and boron. Metal has replaced wood for clubheads, and these metal-woods and irons usually have larger heads to provide a more forgiving hitting area.

Players should be aware that clubs and golf balls must conform to USGA specifications when used in tournaments played under USGA rules. The USGA's policy is to prevent technology from overtaking skill as the major factor in success in golf. The USGA has an equipment testing and research center where special machines are used to make sure that clubs and golf balls conform to the allowed specifications.

Golfing apparel also has changed considerably over the years. During the early days of the sport, many golfers wore knickers, coats, and ties. This mode of dress continued for years, then in the 1920s and '30s slacks replaced the knickers, or plus fours. Coats and ties eventually were replaced by more comfortable shirts and sweaters. Gradually, golfers began to wear more casual clothes, and companies soon began making apparel designed specifically for them.

Knickers and tam-o'-shanter, *left,* were common sights on the course prior to the 1920s. In the 1980s and 1990s, golfing great Payne Stewart (1957–99), *right,* regularly donned the unconventional attire on the course—a reflection of his great respect for the tradition of the game.

Changes and Growth of Golf Courses

Modern golf courses are quite a contrast to those of the 1930s and '40s. Greens often were bumpy, fairways were not always closely mowed, and players seldom knew what to expect from course to course. But even that was far better and different from the earliest courses, which might have been just green patches of grass in a field or pasture.

Many golf courses today, public and private, are well-manicured and beautifully sculptured by professional golf course superintendents. The grass on the greens and fairways is mowed short and tended to daily. The roughs are controlled and maintained to certain heights. Sand bunkers and water hazards are designed not only to add difficulties but also for beauty.

Course architects began building "target" golf courses in the late 1980s and 1990s, but many were considered too difficult for the average player. Target courses usually entail a fairway or green surrounded by hazards such as sand bunkers and water, or waste areas and tall grass. The fairway or green is the target, and players usually have few other good options on where to hit the ball.

Architects began designing more player-friendly layouts. They try to build courses that are visually appealing, and when they cannot incorporate much of the natural terrain, they will use landscaping timbers, create waterfalls, and build mounds, if necessary.

Environmental Concerns

While courses have improved, architects and course superintendents also have had to become more aware of how the environment and wildlife are affected as they build and tend them. In the 1970s, some people became concerned about how the game might be affecting the environment. A series of droughts during the '70s and early '80s resulted in restrictions on the use of potable water by homeowners and businesses in many communities. Golf courses, considered nonessential users of water, were severely restricted.

During the golf course boom of the '80s and '90s, golf courses again were the focus. Concern mounted as to how golf course construction and pesticides affected natural areas. Many of the concerns related to the use of scarce water resources for golf course irrigation, potential water pollution by pesticides and fertilizers, loss of natural areas, and the possible effects of golf course activities on people and wildlife. This brought about increased new studies by several groups, including the USGA and the Golf Course Superintendents Association of America.

The USGA and GCSAA have funded several research projects over the years, and as a result, new grasses that use less water and need fewer chemicals and pesticides have been developed. Course superintendents have implemented better management of the chemicals and pesticides, and studies are continuing. Most new golf course plans must conform to local, state, or national environmental statutes before building can begin.

Golf Lingo

Becoming familiar with the language of golf is part of the game and makes it more fun, too. Some of the more common golf terms are explained below.

ace. A score of 1 on a hole. Also called a *hole-in-one.*

address. The position a player assumes when preparing to hit the ball, either a full shot or a putt.

approach. A shot hit toward the green or hole.

apron. The short grass that surrounds a green and separates it from the fairway or rough. Also called *fringe, frog hair,* or *collar.*

backspin. A reverse rotation of the ball.

backswing. The backward movement of the golf club and body away from the ball; the coiling action before beginning the downswing.

break. The curve of the ball down the slope of the green. To be a proficient putter, a golfer must learn to read the break on the greens.

bump-and-run. A chip shot that is designed to roll, or run, farther than it travels in the air.

bunker. A depression in the ground that usually is filled with sand. There also are grass bunkers.

caddie. A person who carries a player's bag of clubs and sometimes advises the player. Also *"caddy."*

chip. A shot that rolls father than it travels in the air and usually is hit from near the green onto the green.

clubface. The surface of the clubhead that is designed to strike the golf ball.

A **birdie** is a score that is 1-under-par for a hole. For instance, a 2 on a par-3 hole.

A **bogey** is a score that is 1-over-par for a hole. For instance, a 4 on a par-3 hole.

Casual water is a temporary accumulation of water outside of a water hazard that is visible before or after a player takes a stance. Players may take relief (one club length) from casual water, no closer to the hole, without penalty.

Golf Lingo

clubhead. The weighted part of the golf club that makes contact with the golf ball.

colve. A 17th-century Dutch game of hitting an object with a stick.

course management. The use of a plan, or strategy, to best take advantage of a player's weaknesses and strengths to finish a golf course in the fewest number of strokes.

cross-handed. A grip that, for right-handers, puts the left hand below the right. The grip usually is used in putting, but some golfers have played full shots cross-handed.

cup. The metal or plastic sleeve that fits inside the hole on the green and holds the flagstick.

divot. Turf that is torn from the ground, usually during an iron shot that digs into the ground.

dogleg. A hole with a fairway that bends or curves to the right or left. It is so named because it can resemble a dog's hind leg.

downswing. The part of the swing that starts after the backswing, reversing movement toward the ball and target.

draw. A shot that starts the ball on a path to the right of the target, then gently curves back to the left (for a right-handed player) to land at the target.

drive. The first shot off the tee.

duck hook. A shot that curves abruptly and severely right to left for a right-handed player. Also called a *snap hook*.

duffer. An unskilled player.

explosion shot. A shot that removes a large amount of sand, usually from a sand hazard or bunker, to get the ball out. Also called a *blast*.

fade. A slightly curving shot from left to right for a right-handed player.

fairway. The closely mown area between the tee and green.

fairway wood. Even though most fairway woods are made out of metal, they still are called woods. These are any "wood" other than the driver or 1-wood.

fat. Hitting the ground before hitting the ball. Also called *chunking the shot,* or *hitting it thick* or *heavy.*

flagstick. A slender pole, usually about 7 feet tall, that is adorned with a flag and placed inside the cup on the green to mark the location of the hole. It is the preferred name for what many amateurs call the "ping."

An **eagle** is a score of two strokes below par on a hole. For instance, a 3 on a par-5 hole.

Even par is a score that is equivalent to par during, or at the conclusion of, a round of golf.

Golf Lingo

The spectators at a golf tournament or match are called the **gallery**.

Gross score is the actual or unadjusted number of strokes taken to finish a hole or round.

flop shot. A high, soft shot designed to stop quickly when hit to a green.

follow-through. The continuation of a golf swing after the ball has been hit.

fore. A word usually yelled out to warn golfers of a golf ball heading toward them, allowing them to duck or seek cover.

forward press. A slight movement, usually of the hands, arms, or knee, in the direction of the target to initiate the backswing.

grain. The direction the grass blades are growing. The grain can affect the way a ball breaks on a green, especially on Bermuda greens.

green. The most closely mown and smooth area on the course, where the hole is located. Also called the *putting green, putting surface,* or *dance floor.*

green in regulation. When a golfer reaches a green within the prescribed number of strokes. Hitting the green in regulation on a par 3 is one shot; two shots on a par 4; and three shots on a par 5. Often shown as *GIR.*

greens fee. A charge that is paid to play a course.

grip. The handle of a golf club, or the method of holding a golf club.

handicap. A number calculated by specific USGA procedures that is the average difference between a player's scores and a set standard. The number is used so that players of different skill levels can fairly compete against one another.

A **hazard** refers to any bunker or body of water. A body of water usually is marked with either yellow or red stakes or lines, depending on whether it is a regular water hazard or a lateral hazard. A bunker generally is filled with sand, but it also can be filled with grass. A golfer's club cannot touch the ground before hitting a shot out of a hazard or a penalty shot will be incurred.

hole. A 4.5-inch hole in a green into which the ball is to be hit. Also the entire length and vicinity of the playing area from the tee to the green.

hook. The flight path of a golf ball in which the ball starts out to the right (for a right-handed golfer) before curving severely back to the left and missing its target.

knockdown. A shot played with less than a full swing, and usually a shot hit on a lower trajectory than normal. Also called a *punch* or *half shot.*

GOLF LINGO

lag. A putt that is intended to stop close to the hole but is not hit hard enough to roll to the hole or past it.

lateral hazard. A water hazard (whether filled with water or not) that is usually adjacent to, or to the side of, the line of play. It is marked by red stakes or red lines.

lie. The way a ball rests on the ground. It can be a downhill lie, an uphill lie, a fluffy (in taller grass) lie, a good lie, or a bad lie, among others. It also can refer to the number of strokes taken to a current moment on a given hole when the ball is at rest.

left. The backward slant, measured in degrees, of the clubface.

mark. A flat object, usually a coin or plastic piece, used to mark a golf ball's original location after the ball is lifted, usually on a green.

> **Match play** is one player or team against another, playing by holes rather than strokes. The player or team that wins the most holes wins the match. A hole is won by the golfer or team with the fewest strokes on that hole. A player could have the lowest total score over the holes played but lose more holes and thus lose the match.

medallist. The player who has the lowest score, usually in the first round of a tournament or in a qualifier.

mulligan. A second attempt or replay at a shot when the player does not like the result of the first shot. This is not allowed in the "Rules of Golf" but usually is tolerated on the first hole in casual play.

out of bounds. An area that is not part of the golf course and where play is not permitted. It usually is marked by white stakes, lines on the ground, sides of roads, or property fences. If a player hits a ball out-of-bounds, a stroke penalty results and the ball must be played from where the player originally hit it.

pitch. A relatively short, lofted shot designed to land softly and stop quickly. Usually it is hit with a wedge, sand wedge, or lob wedge.

pitch-and-run. A shot near a green that is intended to roll more than it travels in the air. Usually a less-lofted club is used to hit this shot.

pot bunker. A small, deep bunker, typically with steep sides, requiring a very steep angle of ascent to escape.

preferred lies. A local course rule that allows a player to improve his or her lie without penalty. Often used when a course is wet and muddy, or when the fairways are not in good condition. Also called *winter rules* or *improved lies*.

Net score is a player's score after the player's handicap has been applied. If the golfer shoots a gross 82 and has an 8 handicap, his net score is 74.

GOLF LINGO

> A **provisional ball** is an additional shot played when it is believed that the original ball might be out of bounds or lost. The shot should be played after everyone in the group has hit and before leaving the area. To save time, a player will elect to hit a provisional ball when he thinks his ball is out of bounds or lost. Otherwise, the player must return to the tee to hit again.

putt. A shot usually hit with a putter on the putting green. A putter also can be used from off the green.

putter. A club with a fairly straight clubface that is used for rolling, or putting, a golf ball on the ground or green.

rough. Longer grass that is adjacent to the fairways, greens, and perhaps tees. Designed to penalize golfers who are not accurate because it generally is more difficult to hit from the rough.

round. A completed circuit of 18 holes.

> **Rub of the green** usually refers to some odd occurrence, often a bad break, not caused by the player or caddie, for which there is no relief provided by the "Rules of Golf." For example, a ball could hit a cart path and bounce out of bounds or in a hazard whereas had it not hit the cart path, it would have stopped well short of the out of bounds or hazard.

sandbagger. This derogatory term applies to a golfer who lies about his or her ability in order to gain an advantage in a match, tournament, or wager. He or she often posts artificially high scores to inflate his or her handicap.

The term **scratch** applies to a golfer with a 0 handicap. This golfer normally averages par and will have no strokes deducted from the gross score.

sand trap. The common term for a sand-filled bunker. Traps are considered hazards.

skins. A type of competition or wager format where only the low score among a set group of players can win the hole. If more than one person ties for low score, no one wins a skin. Usually the bet, or skin, carries over when there is a tie on a hole.

slice. A wildly curving shot from left to right for a right-handed player. Also known as a *banana ball,* this is the prevalent shot among beginners.

stroke. The act of swinging a club, including the putter, with the intention of hitting a golf ball.

stroke-and-distance. This is a penalty in certain circumstances, including—for example—hitting a ball out of bounds. The golfer must hit again from the original spot and incur a stroke penalty.

sweet spot. The perfect point on the clubface to strike a golf ball to make an accurate shot.

20   GOLF

swing plane. The plane, or arc, that the shaft of the club or the clubhead takes during the swing. Usually described as being flat or upright; often determines the flight of the ball.

tee box. The group of teeing grounds. It includes multiple sets of tee markers.

tee markers. Two objects that indicate the forward boundary of the teeing ground. Players cannot hit from in front of the markers without incurring a penalty. Also called *tee blocks*. "Markers" also may refer to those who serve as scorers in competitions.

tee shot. The first shot on a hole.

unplayable lie. A player may determine that the ball cannot be played from its current location and deem it unplayable. After taking relief under the "Rules of Golf," the player will incur a one-stroke penalty.

up-and-down. This term is used when a golfer is able to hole the ball in two shots from off the green, usually by a chip and one putt.

waggle. To make small back-and-forth movements of the clubhead before grounding the club on the approach shot.

yardage. This usually applies when a golfer wants to know how many yards it is to the green from where he or she is hitting. Some courses have yardage markers or yardage books to help the golfer. Knowing the yardage helps the golfer decide which club to hit.

yips. Generally, a nervous twitching during a putting stroke that causes inconsistent results. Some golfers blame their poor putting on "having the yips."

The term **through the green** is used when a particular rule applies everywhere except the green being played. For example, the term might be used if players are allowed to lift, clean, and place their golf balls "through the green" because of muddy conditions; they would not be allowed to do so otherwise.

Stroke play means scoring by the total number of strokes during a round. Also called *medal play*.

The **teeing ground** is the starting point for the hole. This rectangular area is defined by one set of tee markers.

= Tools of the Game

Tools of the Game

In addition to having a good, reliable swing to produce long, accurate tee shots, golfers should have clubs that match their swing. That means having clubs with the proper shaft, grip size, and swing weight for the golfer. If a golfer is equipped with a poorly fitted or ill-maintained club, even a good swing might not produce good shots.

Other golfing equipment also could enhance the game of even a novice golfer, including the choice of ball and the clothing worn on the course.

Clubs

Choosing golf clubs can be somewhat complicated. When choosing a set of clubs, a golfer must consider such elements as the different types and shapes of clubheads; the length of the club shafts, which have different flexes and are made from different materials such as steel or graphite; the total weight of each club; and the size of the grips.

A golf professional can help a player determine what types of clubs and shafts might be appropriate for his or her swing. Golf equipment can be bought, and usually can be tested, at golf courses and/or golf specialty stores.

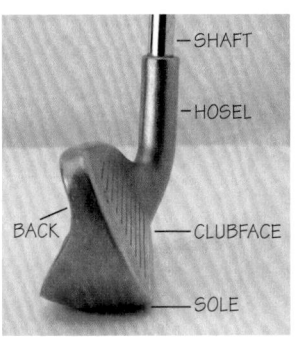

GOLF 23

TOOLS OF THE GAME

Irons

Irons

Irons have clubfaces made of steel with a relatively narrow sole—the bottom of the clubhead. The most commonly used irons are numbered from 2 to 9, with the lower-numbered clubs used to achieve shots of longer length and less height than the higher-numbered ones. Some irons are used for pitching, chipping, and hitting out of bunkers, including the pitching wedge, sand wedge, and lob wedge. There are some specialty irons designed for chipping.

Loft is a term used to indicate the backward slant, or angle, of the clubface. It is measured in degrees. All golf clubs have some loft, but each one varies according to its use.

Wedges

Wedges are called "short" irons and have the greatest loft. It's best to use these clubs for greater accuracy, for distances under 130 yards. Wedges will hit the ball up relatively high and generally land without a lot of roll. They are especially helpful for getting out of bunkers. The gap wedge was introduced to fill the "loft" gap between the pitching wedge and sand wedge.

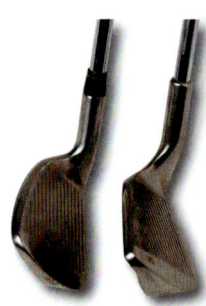

Wedges

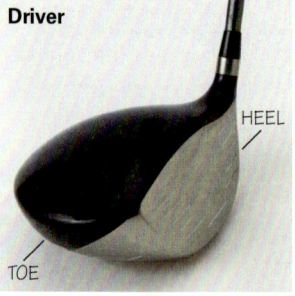

Driver — HEEL, TOE

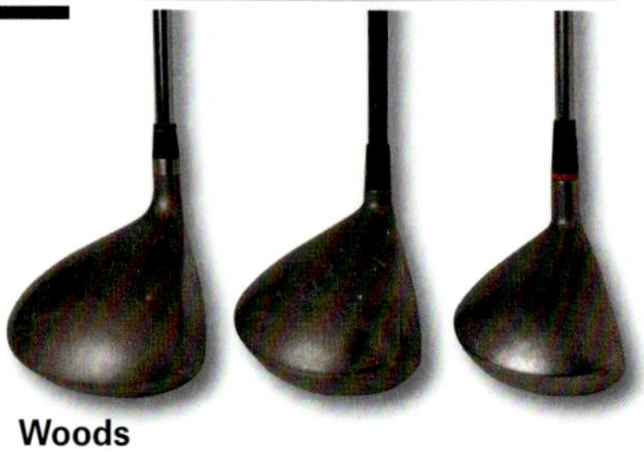

Woods

Woods

Woods have larger clubheads than irons and have longer shafts. Originally these clubheads were made of wood, but in recent years they have been replaced by different types of metal. Woods range from the driver to fairway woods such as the 3-wood and up to a 7-wood. As with the numbered irons, the lower the number of the wood, the longer the shot will travel with the least amount of loft. The driver is the longest club, featuring a clubface with the least loft of all clubs. It is designed to hit the ball for distance.

24 GOLF

Putters

Usually used on the greens, putters come in all shapes and sizes, featuring almost flat clubfaces that allow the golf ball to be rolled close to the ground. Most golfers will try several putters before carrying one that feels right for them.

Hybrid Club

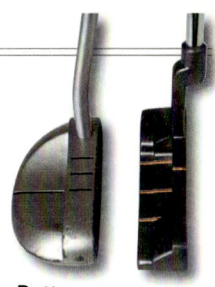

Putters

Also called a utility club, the hybrid club combines elements of both a wood and an iron into a single club. Most hybrid clubs are designed to replace the 2-, 3-, 4-, and 5-irons. Many golfers think the hybrid clubs are easier to hit than those irons because the hybrid combines the forgiveness, distance, and height of a fairway wood and the stopping ability of an iron, which adds up to the golfer's sense of having greater control and accuracy. Hybrid clubs are sold as hybrid "sets," or as individual clubs, such as the aptly named "rescue" club, which helps rescue players from the rough.

Although the "Rules of Golf" allow you to carry any mixture of 14 clubs in your bag, you can carry fewer if you like. Many golfers think the game is based on three scoring clubs: driver, wedge, and putter. A "short" set consists of six clubs: 3-wood, 3-, 5-, 7-, and 9-irons, and a putter. A "full" set has 12 clubs: driver, 3- and 5-fairway woods, 3-, 4-, 5-, 6-, 7-, 8-, and 9-irons, a pitching wedge, and a putter. Most golfers include a sand wedge with the short or full set.

Other Accessories

Golf Ball. Golf balls have varying covers, including balata (a natural rubber) and various synthetics. Balata gives a softer feel but cuts easier. Newer synthetic covers also offer softer feels and usually are more durable than balata. Golf balls come with either a wound or a solid core. Wound golf balls usually have a small rubber ball filled with liquid in the center and wound with narrow rubber bands. More common are solid golf balls, which are created from two solid pieces that are compressed together.

Golf towel and golf balls

Multilayer balls have a solid core and a soft outer cover, separated by ultra-thick layers of various materials. While these balls offer good performance in distance, durability, spin, and feel, they are very expensive. Ask your merit badge counselor or a golf retail specialist for assistance with choosing the right kind of golf ball for your playing style and ability.

TOOLS OF THE GAME

Tees. These wooden or plastic pegs are designed to cradle the ball for the golfer's tee shot. Different lengths of tees help golfers consistently tee the ball to a desired height.

Ball Marker. These flat, usually plastic objects are used to replace a golf ball on greens either to prevent blocking the shot of another player or to allow the golfer to pick up the ball and clean it. The golf ball then replaces the marker in the exact location.

Divot Tool. These usually metal, horseshoe-shaped objects are used to repair turf. With the two metal points, a golfer can "stitch" the grass together where there is a ball mark and then smooth the repaired area with the flat part of a putter.

Golf Towel. Many golfers attach a partially wet towel to their golf bag and use it to help clean off golf balls or clubheads during a round. In hot weather, some golfers carry another towel to keep sweat out of their eyes and off their hands and arms.

Club Covers. While irons usually do not require covers, most golfers use covers to protect their metal woods. Probably more important to golfers when woods were actually made of wood, club covers help reduce scratches or dents to club metal. They come in many different materials and designs, including shaped as animal heads and decorated in collegiate logos.

Golf Bag. While most touring professionals use a large, heavy bag, they have someone else carrying it. For a player who carries his or her own bag, several lightweight bags are available, and a double shoulder strap makes it easier on the back and more comfortable to carry. Bags should have enough pockets to carry such incidentals as rain gear, golf balls, tees, divot tool, pencil, ball marker, golf glove, and rulebook. Oh, and don't forget the sunscreen. Young golfers might consider other accessories, including a stroke counter that can be clicked after each stroke, which could make keeping score much easier.

Among some of the necessary accessories for the golf game and protection of equipment are golf balls, club covers, tees, ball markers, and a divot tool.

Maintenance and Care of Golf Clubs

Golfers should keep the golf club grips—their only contact with the club—and clubheads clean and in good condition. Slick or worn grips can cause hands to slip, resulting in errant shots. Many pro shops or golf specialty stores have grip-cleaning products, though daily cleaning usually can be handled with warm water and a towel. Kits are available to allow golfers to change their own grips when necessary, though most pro shops or golf specialty stores will change the grips for a relatively small fee.

It also is important to keep the clubfaces and clubhead grooves clean. A clubhead can be cleaned with a towel and water, and the grooves, which help produce the backspin on a golf ball, usually can be cleaned using the sharp end of a tee.

Apparel

Golf Shoes. These come in several styles and colors with either leather or synthetic tops. Most golf shoes are available with nonmetal spikes, which many golf courses now require. Golf shoes with nonmetal spikes are lighter and generally more comfortable.

Golf Gloves. Normally the better gloves are made of leather. A right-handed golfer usually wears the glove on the left hand, and the left-handed golfer wears one on the right hand. Gloves usually help a golfer grip the club, though some great golfers, such as Ben Hogan, never wore one. It is important to keep them as dry as possible during use and to allow them to dry fully after a round. Conditioners can be used to help prolong the life of leather gloves.

Clubs and Accessories for Junior Golfers

Besides taking lessons from a qualified golf teacher, obtaining correct-fitting clubs is considered very important to any golfer, beginner or expert.

A common practice among parents is to equip their children in cut-down adult golf clubs. Most teaching and club professionals advise against this, because when a shaft is cut down, the weight of the clubhead becomes heavier and the flex changes. Professionals say that neither change would be appropriate for a junior and could lead to bad swing habits.

Professionals recommend buying clubs designed for juniors. A golfer can be fitted for the correct size according to height and age. Normally, a junior should be fit for clubs that are 2 to 4 inches longer than what would be normal for his or her current height. This would assure that the clubs would not become too small in a short time as the player grows. It usually is a good idea to let a qualified professional watch the junior swing before obtaining a final fitting.

How to Play the Game

As equipment has changed, so has the swing. When golfers played with wooden-shafted clubs, the clubheads usually had to be fanned open on the backswing and then closed coming through the ball because of the torque in the shafts. Swings were flatter than the more upright swings of today. A flat swing is more around the body, much like a baseball swing might be. An upright swing is more up and down rather than around.

When steel shafts were introduced in the 1930s, players began changing to a more upright swing with less hip turn and the left foot staying closer to, or on, the ground. Golfers were able to swing harder while maintaining accuracy.

Even though instructors may teach certain methods to swing a club, there is no absolute way to swing. A look at many of the top players over the years proves that. Many, such as David Duval, Jim Furyk, and Fred Couples, employ swings that would not fit many of the new methods.

However, knowing certain fundamentals can make playing golf easier. The object is to develop a consistent setup procedure and swing. Although golfers can try to learn how to swing by reading and looking at pictures, it is recommended that they take lessons from a qualified instructor.

Note: Left-handers should reverse all the instructions listed.

Approximately 8 to 10 percent of golfers in America are left-handed. In 2003, Mike Weir was the first lefty to win the Masters. Then Phil Mickelson, another lefty, won the Masters the following year.

Assessing the Shot

Finding the grip and swing that works for you is critical for becoming a consistent player. Watch the world's best players on the professional golf tours and you will see that there are different grips and swings. They are proof that there is more than one way to grip and swing a club. These players have practiced long hours to find what works for them.

Some basics need to be observed, but each golfer should experiment to find which grip works best and to build a consistent swing.

The Grip

Because the player's hands are the only contact with a golf club, the grip is critical to constructing a consistent golf game. Three grips are widely used: the Vardon (or overlapping) grip, the interlocking grip, and the full-fingered (often called the baseball or 10-fingered) grip. Whichever grip is used, the hands should be close together and more or less parallel so that they can best work together.

Vardon Grip

Hold the club diagonally in the palm of the left hand and close the fingers so that the shaft lies diagonally across the second joint of the index finger. Close the hand with the thumb positioned slightly to the right of the top of the shaft. The V that is formed by the thumb and forefinger should point toward the right shoulder. Now move the right hand over the shaft with the left thumb fitting inside the palm of the right hand. The little finger of the right hand should overlap the left index finger or behind it. The club should be held with most pressure on the last three fingers of the left hand and middle two fingers of the right hand.

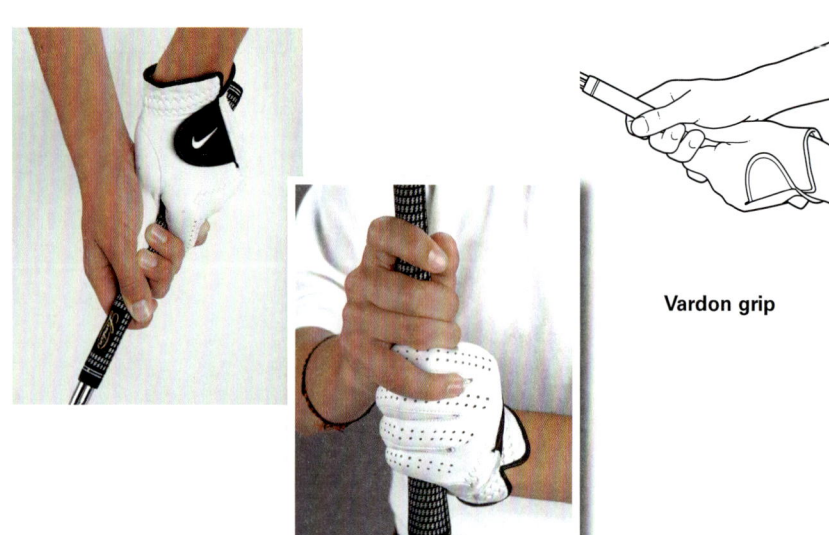

Vardon grip

How to Play the Game

Interlocking Grip

The interlocking grip is similar to the Vardon grip, except that instead of overlapping the little finger of the right hand, it interlocks with the index finger of the left hand.

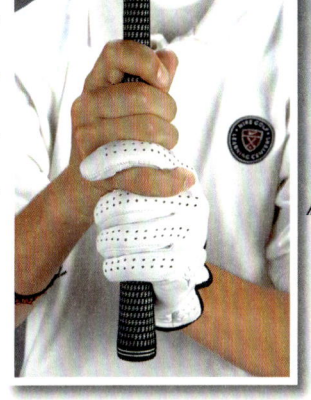

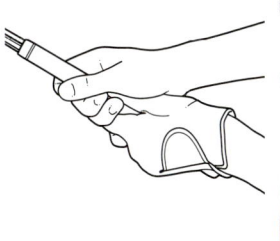

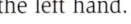
Interlocking grip

Full-Fingered Grip

Although the Vardon and interlocking grips are considered best for allowing the hands to work together, many outstanding players have used the full-fingered grip. The grip is taken the same way as the other two, but all fingers remain on the shaft. The little finger of the right hand does not overlap or interlock.

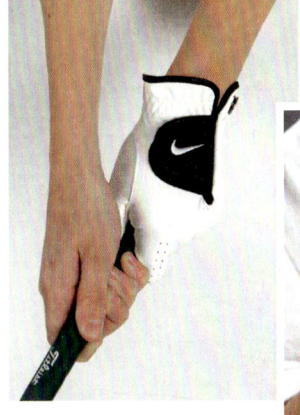

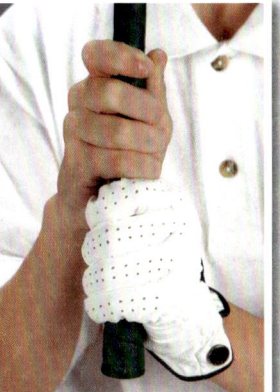

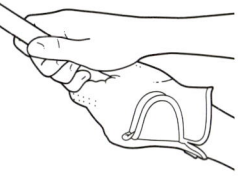

Full-fingered grip

GOLF   31

The Stance

Before taking a stance to hit the golf ball, a player should have assessed the upcoming shot and selected a club.

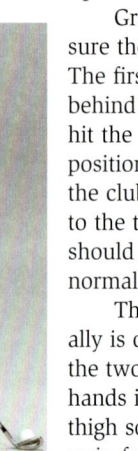

Grip the club and check to make sure the clubface is square to the ball. The first action should be setting the club behind the ball along the line you want to hit the ball. This should be done before positioning the feet and body. After placing the club, position your feet and body square to the target. The feet, shoulders, and hips should be perpendicular to the target on a normal shot.

The ball position for normal shots usually is on a line an equal distance between the two feet. Grip the club and position the hands in a line with the inside of your left thigh so that the hands are slightly ahead, or in front, of the ball.

Flex your knees, bend slightly from the hips, and keep a straight spine. Your chin should be up enough to allow the left shoulder to turn underneath. One way to check your stance is to imagine a vertical line descending down the middle of your right shoulder, through your kneecap, and into the ball of your right foot.

The square stance

How to Play the Game

This is a square stance, which helps a golfer swing back the clubhead along the intended line to produce a straight shot. An open stance, with the feet, shoulders, and hips positioned slightly to the left of the ball, helps promote an outside-in swing to produce a fade or slice—a ball that might start straight and turn right.

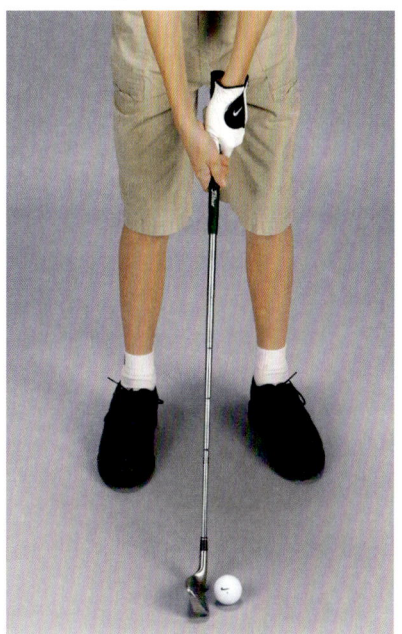 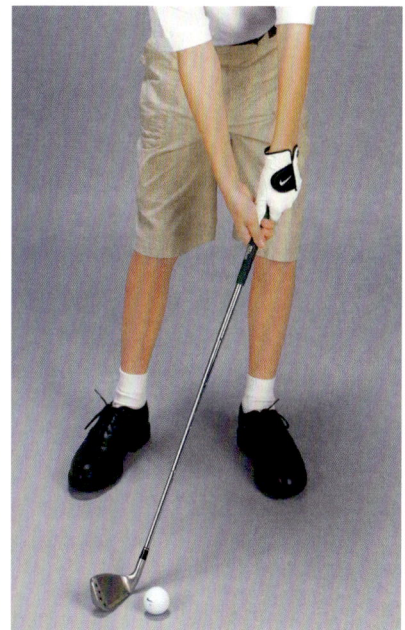

Hands at address: correct *(left)* and incorrect *(right)*

The object of the swing is to lead the clubhead into the ball with your hands. Usually the hands should be about 6 inches from your body. This helps set your shoulders in a position to turn more easily on a fairly upright plane.

Left Arm

To help develop a consistent, repeating swing, a golfer should set up for shots in a certain pattern. One checkpoint is that, at address, the left arm and club shaft should be in about the same line. The left wrist should form a slight angle. An unnatural flat or straight left wrist can impede the hinging of the wrists.

Right Side

A full coil of the upper body is necessary to achieve distance for full shots. To help achieve the coil, you should relax the right side and right arm at address. If the right side is tense, it is harder to achieve a coil.

Right Shoulder

Your right shoulder should naturally be lower than your left at address. However, this should be checked, especially if you are slicing the ball. Holding the right shoulder lower than the left helps to move the shoulder on the backswing on a more vertical plane. If the right shoulder is too high, you could hit from the outside and slice the ball.

Safety

To keep yourself and those around you out of harm's way along the golf course, practice these safety precautions:

- When swinging a club, either at the ball or practicing, be far enough away from other players to avoid hitting anyone. Do not hit the ball into the group playing ahead of you. Make sure the players are out of the way before anyone in your group tees off.

- Yell "Fore!" if your shot is heading for someone, either in front of you or on adjacent holes.

Starting the Swing

Many golfers like to waggle the club to stay loose before starting their backswing. They also like some type of action, sometimes called a forward or stationary press, to begin the backswing. A press can include slightly moving the hands forward, cocking the head, or slightly bending the right knee.

When waggling the club back and forth, some golfers will waggle the clubhead outside the line of flight if they are trying to hit a fade or waggle it inside the line of flight if trying to hit a hook. Many instructors say the takeaway should be in one piece. In other words, the entire left side must move together, or in one piece, to begin the backswing.

Another way to start is to imagine your navel turning to your right. More modern swings try limiting the hip turn while fully coiling the shoulders, which builds up tension. However, a person needs to be very flexible and strong to perfect this swing. Basically, the hips should turn when the shoulders force them. As they turn no farther than the shoulders, the left knee will turn in and point to the ball.

Backswing Turn

Turn the shoulders to swing the clubhead back. Golfers who lift the club with their hands and arms can create several problems in the swing. Your weight should still feel as if it is on the inside of your feet as you shift most of your weight back to your right foot. Any swaying will throw your swing off plane and make it difficult to return to the ball with consistency.

When the shoulder turn moves the club to about hip height, the wrists begin cocking as the club continues upward. The right arm should not fly out or stay so close to the body as to restrict the backswing. Try to coil the shoulders as far as possible and still maintain balance while imagining that your hips are turning in a barrel.

Top of the Swing

When the club reaches the top, you should be coiled and ready to deliver a strong downswing toward the ball. The club should be parallel to the target line. A shaft that crosses the line (pointing left of the target) will cause a swing that is too far inside, and a shaft that is "laid off" (pointing right of the target) will cause a swing that is too far outside the line.

Length of the backswing will vary with a golfer's flexibility and ability. Basically, the right knee should remain flexed, and the left foot should not raise excessively off the ground. You should not sway back on your left leg or foot, and the grip should remain firm.

The clubface alignment at the top might also dictate the type of shot you will hit. If the clubface is open (the toe pointing to the ground), you might slice; if it is closed (clubface facing skyward), you might hook. Square is considered somewhere in between. However, many good golfers have had open and closed clubfaces, so there is no absolute.

Downswing

The downswing is largely a reflex action of the backswing, but your weight should begin shifting to the left side with the shoulders and arms following. With the weight shifting to the left foot, the knees begin moving fast toward the direction of the shot. During the lateral slide of the knees, the hips should be turning to the left to clear a path to swing the club along the target line.

A major fault is starting the downswing with the hands and arms before the legs and hips have begun to move. But it also is possible to overuse the legs and hips. Another key to having a consistent swing is maintaining your spine angle throughout the swing. This prevents bobbing up and down during the swing.

Modern instructors are teaching a flatter finish and straighter back as you continue through the ball, rather than the reverse C, which marked Jack Nicklaus' strong swing. Also, a flatter finish is regarded as being better for your back.

Full Shot From the Tee

The basic principles of the grip, stance, backswing, and downswing apply for all swings, including the drive. A swing with a driver is more of a sweeping action. It probably is better to tee the ball higher rather than too low so that the driver strikes it at the bottom of the swing or slightly on the upswing. One good measurement is to have the top of the clubface level with the ball's equator when the club is grounded.

The Tee Box

Every hole begins with a teeing ground, from which you will hit your drive or tee shot. The teeing ground is two club lengths deep. Its width is defined by a set of tee markers. You must tee up your ball between the markers. The teeing ground refers to one set of markers, but there are multiple sets of markers, which correspond to different yardages. These markers are called forward, middle, and back tees. The forward tees are the shortest set; the back tees are the longest. This group of teeing grounds is called a tee box. Some courses have more than three teeing grounds in the tee boxes. Play the forward tees until you understand how far you can consistently drive the ball, then play from the markers that best suit your game.

THE FULL SWING

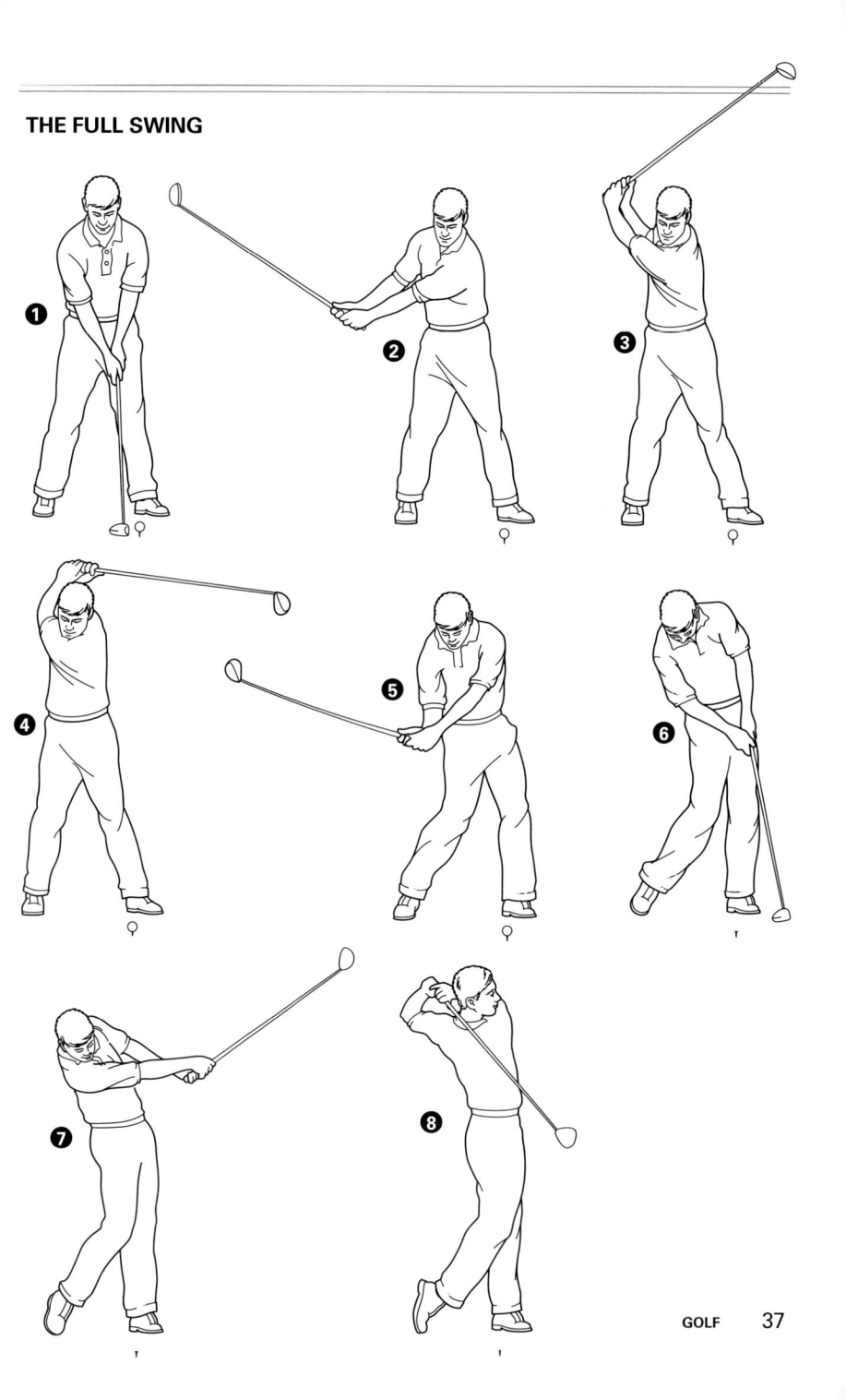

The ball position normally will be a couple of inches inside the left heel. Turning out the left foot may help clear the way for the hands and arms on the downswing.

Hit through the ball, not at it, and, if the left side leads as it should, you should be able to swing your arms and hands through the ball as hard as possible. Extend your right arm as you hit through the ball. To accomplish the speed through the ball, it is important not to swing too fast going back. Swinging back too fast can destroy the timing needed to deliver a hard blow.

Using Fairway Clubs

The shot from the fairway with a metal wood is slightly different from the drive. Generally, a 3- or 4-wood is used from the fairways, and the 5- to 7-woods are used to dig the ball out of roughs. The swing is virtually as it is with a driver, but there is more of a downward blow to the ball to make sure the ball gets off the ground. The ball position will be slightly behind where you would place the ball for a drive.

Irons

A 2- or 3-iron is longer than a 7- or 9-iron, but it does not mean you have to swing harder to hit it. Irons can be more intimidating, though, because they have straighter faces and, generally, smaller heads.

The stance will be wider than it is with short irons, and the arc will be longer because the shaft is longer. This will create more clubhead speed.

Usually, long irons should be used off tees and in fairways. It is difficult to hit long irons out of roughs. A 4-, 5-, or 7-wood would be a better choice from the rough. The ball position will be similar as with the fairway woods, a good shoulder turn is important, and the swing will be more of a sweeping one rather than a downward blow as it would be with short irons.

It is better to hit with more of a downward blow with the short irons because you usually are trying to stop the ball as quickly as possible on the green. The downward blow will impart more backspin and allow the ball to stop sooner. Put the

> Hitting a long iron is similar to hitting a driver. Determine on the practice tee how far you can hit the ball in the air consistently with all irons.

ball back more in the middle of the stance in order to hit it with a more downward strike. The ball should be hit first and the divot will be taken in front of the ball as you swing through.

Specialty Shots

While it would be nice if you could swing the same way each time, there may be occasions when you need to hit a low shot, a high shot, a hook, or a slice.

To hit the ball low, choke down on the grip an inch or two and move the ball back in your stance more toward the right foot. Move your hands ahead of the ball, swing shorter, lead down with your hands, and restrict your follow-through.

To hit it high, play the ball more toward the left foot and position the hands more even with the ball. Stay behind the ball during the swing. You still hit down and through.

To draw or hook the ball, move the ball back in the stance, close your stance by drawing the right foot back 2 to 3 inches, and position the hands slightly ahead of the ball. Take the club back more inside, or on-line with the way your feet are now aligned, and make your regular swing. If you need a more severe hook, close the blade as much as you deem necessary.

To fade or slice the ball, open your stance by drawing the left foot back 2 or 3 inches. Position the ball either just off the left heel or an inch back toward the middle. Take the club a little outside the line to slightly cut across the line to promote a left-to-right shot. If a more severe slice is needed, open the blade of the club.

Be sure to practice all these shots and experiment with ball and hand positioning so that you will know what works for you.

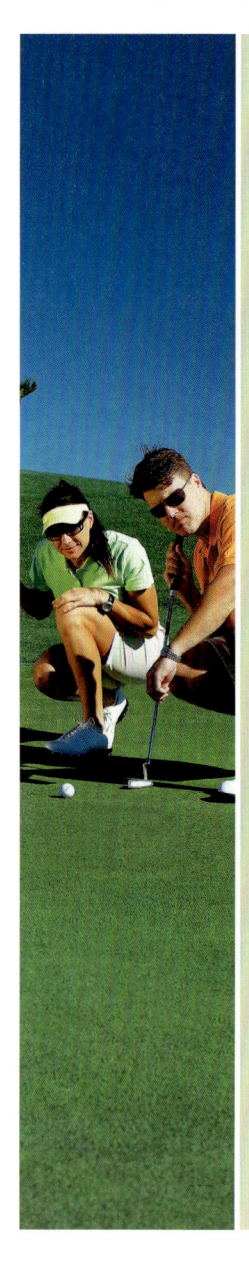

Scoring and Handicaps

Handicaps in golf are used to help make competition more fair among players of different abilities. A handicap index is the USGA's method to indicate a measurement of a player's potential scoring ability on a course of standard difficulty.

A handicap index is issued by a specific golf club and is determined using a player's after scores from multiple rounds of golf. It determines the number of strokes a golfer receives to adjust the gross score. The USGA prefers that a minimum of 20 scores be submitted to determine a handicap index. As a player continues to submit scores, the handicap probably will fluctuate.

To figure out your unofficial handicap, you must first determine the handicap differentials on 10 of your last 20 scores, as follows.

Step 1—Subtracting the USGA course rating from the adjusted gross score.

Step 2—Multiply the difference by 113 (the slope rating of a course of standard difficulty).

Step 3—Divide that number by the USGA slope rating and round to the nearest tenth.

Step 4—Find the average of the 10 differentials, and multiply the average by 0.96.

Step 5—Delete all numbers after tenths, but do not round to the nearest tenth.

The result is your handicap index. The handicap index is then compared to the course's handicap chart to determine a player's handicap for that course.

How to Play the Game

Short Game

Having a strong short game can be the fastest way to lower your scores. Seldom does a golfer hit all 18 greens in regulation, so chipping and putting become a critical part of scoring.

Putting

One area of golf in which styles are vastly different is putting. Golfers sometimes go to extreme lengths to find a dependable, reliable stroke that can work under pressure. In the past few years, some players have switched to a cross-handed style or something more unorthodox, have used long putters that wedge against the chest, and have tried every putter shape on the market.

Golfers once used a lot of wrist when they putted over what were often slower and bumpier greens. Today's players usually try to eliminate as much wrist movement as possible and use arms and shoulders in their stroke.

One of the first things a golfer must do is find the "sweet spot" on the putter. This usually is in the center of the putter face. Balls that are putted on the toe or heel of the face usually will not be solid strikes and will cause erratic results. The hands should form an extension of the club, and they can help strike the ball square by using a palm-to-palm grip.

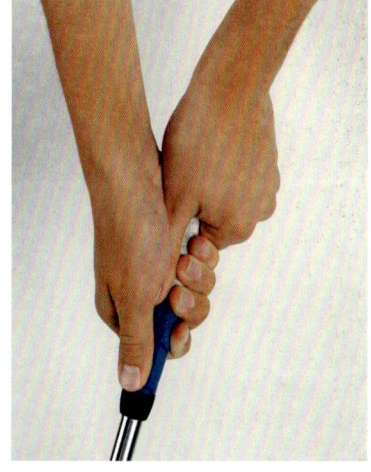

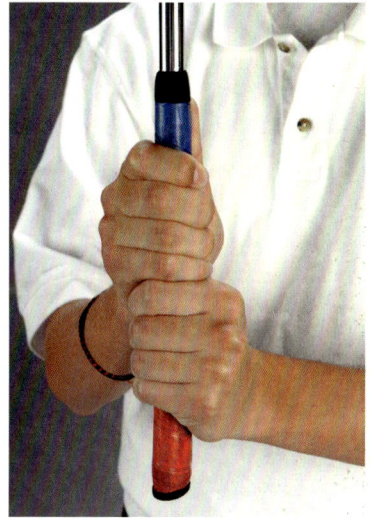

Palm-to-palm grip

GOLF 41

How to Play the Game

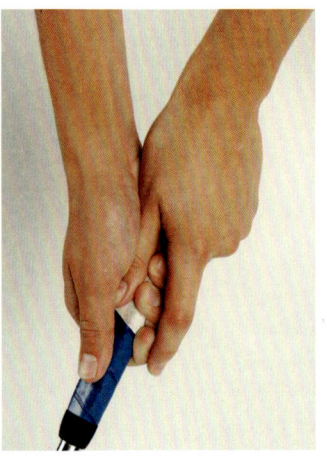

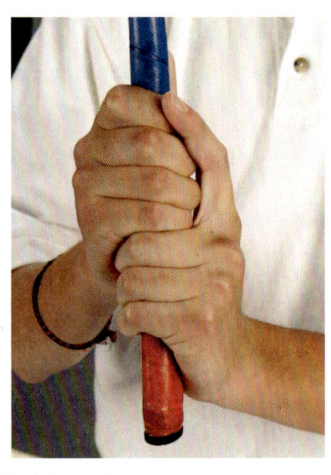

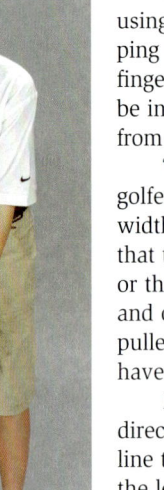

Reverse overlapping grip

One of the most common putting grips involves using a reverse overlapping. This involves overlapping the left index finger down the first three or four fingers of the right hand. Most of the pressure should be in the left hand to help prevent that hand and wrist from breaking down during the downstroke.

The putting stance, which varies widely from golfer to golfer, usually has the feet about shoulder width with the arms hanging down comfortably so that they will not be restricted on either the backswing or the downswing. The feet can be square to the line and open (left foot pulled back) or closed (right foot pulled back). There have been excellent putters who have used each.

Most golfers believe it is critical to have the eyes directly over the ball in order to see a more accurate line to the hole. Most play the ball on a line opposite the left heel with the hands either even or just slightly ahead of the ball. Try to keep the stroke as smooth as possible, maybe even trying a one-two count: The backswing is the count of one, and the stroke and follow-through is two.

Putting stance

How to Play the Game

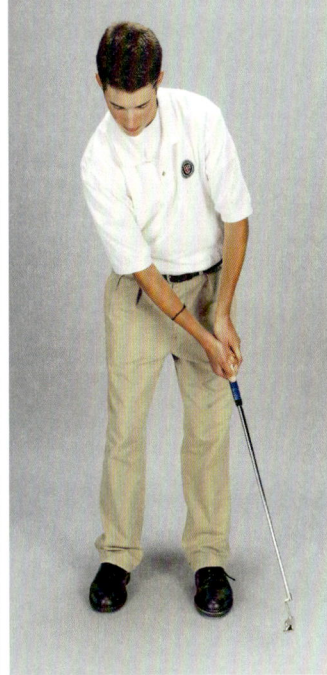

The backswing count

The stroke and follow-through, count two

Johnny Miller, World Golf Hall of Famer and TV broadcaster, bases his one-two count on the speed of the stroke as he calculates it after examining the putt. He tries to visualize the line from the ball to the hole, taking in to account any break of the green, and the distance to the hole. He then sets the blade of the putter behind the ball that faces the line and strokes with the hands following down the line.

Professional golfers and top amateurs normally have a pattern of addressing the ball. For example, Miller looks at the putt from behind and visualizes the line of the putt to the hole. Then he steps up to the ball, places the putter on-line, takes his stance, takes one look at the hole, looks back to the putter to check his alignment, and then takes a second look at the hole to get a feel for the distance. The moment he looks back at the putter is when he begins drawing back his putter. Being systematic, he said, keeps your attitude positive and helps your mind to visualize making the putt.

How to Play the Game

For more information about golf camps, schools, tournaments, and college-playing opportunities, see the resources section.

Dave Pelz, a golf instructor who specializes in the short game and is an adviser for several top players, has his own method for putting. He also has devised drills that help golfers develop a feel for putting. One is a short-putt drill. He said the best way to sink short putts is to hit them firmly, at a force that would cause the ball to roll 17 inches past the hole if it missed.

He says you should practice this by hitting one ball from 3 feet, one from 4 feet, and one from 5 feet, and repeat the process from two other sides of the cup. After making all your putts from all three sides, he suggests trying this with your eyes closed after lining up the putts.

Another is the 20-foot drill. Putt 20-foot putts in groups of three from opposite directions of the hole until you can stop 10 shots in a row within one putter length of the back edge of the hole without leaving any putt short.

Then there is the lag-putt drill. On putts longer than 40 feet, try to lag the ball to the hole—get as close as you can to the hole without going past it. Stroke three putts each from 40, 60, and 50 feet and try to stop the ball within 4, 6, and 5 feet, respectively.

Pelz recommends that golfers devote more of their practice time on the short game, noting that a golfer who shoots 70 will average about 30 strokes with his putter, and most who shoot 85 will use the putter about 35 times.

Golf is a sport you can enjoy for the rest of your life. These days you may golf for fun with a family member or friend. Later you might decide to try out for a position on a high school or college team, or play golf to build business relationships, or just to relax. In any case, you can always improve your game.

One exciting element of golf is that no two courses are identical; landscapes vary. Many golfers think the battle is between the player and the course. Although most golfers expect to compare their scores to other players, they can also play a course again and again, comparing their personal scores for different rounds to appreciate their own improvement against the course.

In playing golf, you will learn much about yourself. Golf teaches you to be humble and more patient, to have respect for other players and the course, and to be courteous. If you want to improve your game, you will work to develop social skills, self-discipline, and mental toughness.

RIVERSIDE GOLF CLUB

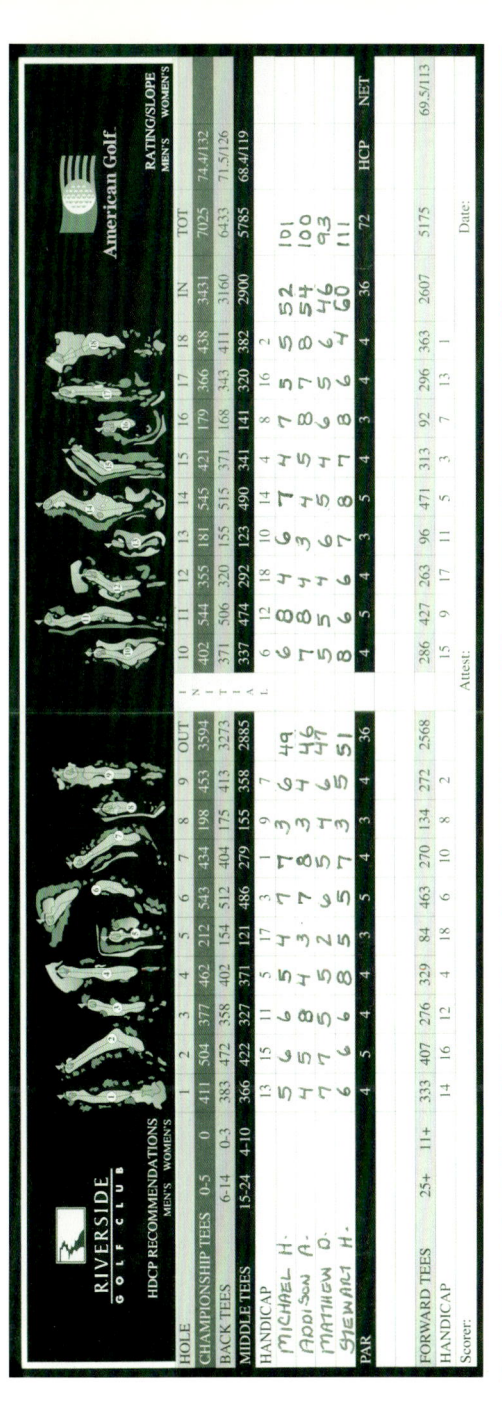

American Golf

HDCP RECOMMENDATIONS	MEN'S	WOMEN'S

											RATING/SLOPE	
											MEN'S	WOMEN'S

HOLE	1	2	3	4	5	6	7	8	9	OUT	10	11	12	13	14	15	16	17	18	IN	TOT		
CHAMPIONSHIP TEES 0-5 0	411	504	377	462	212	543	434	198	453	3594	402	544	355	181	545	421	179	366	438	3431	7025	74.4/132	
BACK TEES 6-14 0-3	383	472	358	402	154	512	404	175	413	3273	371	506	320	155	515	371	168	343	411	3160	6433	71.5/126	
MIDDLE TEES 15-24 4-10	366	422	327	371	121	486	279	155	358	2885	337	474	292	123	490	341	141	320	382	2900	5785	68.4/119	
HANDICAP	13	15	11	5	17	3	1	9	7		6	12	18	10	14	4	8	16	2				
MICHAEL H.	5	5	6	5	4	7	7	3	6	49	6	8	4	6	7	4	7	5	5	52	101		
ADDISON A.	4	5	5	4	3	7	8	3	4	46	7	8	4	3	7	5	8	7	8	54	100		
MATTHEW O.	7	7	5	5	2	5	5	1	5	47	5	5	4	6	5	4	5	7	6	46	93		
STEWART H.	6	6	4	8	5	7	3	5	3	51	8	6	6	7	8	4	6	6	4	60	111		
PAR	4	5	4	4	3	5	4	3	4	36	4	5	4	3	5	4	3	4	4	36	72	HCP	NET
FORWARD TEES 25+ 11+	333	407	276	329	84	463	270	134	272	2568	286	427	263	96	471	313	92	296	363	2607	5175	69.5/113	
HANDICAP	14	16	12	4	18	6	10	8	2		15	9	17	11	5	3	7	13	1				

Scorer: _____ Attest: _____ Date: _____

The Course Scorecard

Using the course scorecard is required in tournament play. Typical cards have a line for the golfer's name on the left side and a grid with boxes to record scores for all 18 course holes. The pars for each hole also are shown on the card. In competition, a golfer's score for each hole is entered in the corresponding space. The golfer is not required to total the scores for either set of nine holes or the 18-hole round, but for the card to be official, the player and his scorekeeper must verify the scores and sign the card. In competition play, a golfer does not record his own scores.

Chip-and-Run Shot

Use a straighter-faced club, such as a 6- or 7-iron, for a chip-and-run shot. The object is to hit the ball a short distance in the air and then let it roll on the green as much as possible. This usually is the best shot when the ball is just off the green and the pin is several feet or yards away.

The chip-and-run shot, beginning stance *(left)* and follow-through *(right)*

Generally, the ball will roll two-thirds of the distance to the pin, so try to select a spot on the green to land the ball about a third of the distance to the pin. This distance will vary according to the green and the club that is used. Open the stance, choke down on the club a couple of inches, position the ball slightly back in the stance, and position the hands ahead of the ball. The club is taken back with the arms and hands with very little wrist action and with little or no movement of the body. Come through firmly with the arms and hands and finish directly toward the hole.

Lob and Pitch Shots

These shots are performed with a more lofted club, such as a wedge, lob wedge, or sand wedge. This shot is commonly used when the pin is located nearer the ball and there is not much green to hit to.

To hit a lob shot, a high shot that should stop quickly, position the ball off your left heel and open your stance by moving the feet, hips, and shoulders to the left. Take a fairly wide stance and flex your knees. Keep them flexed throughout the shot. Do not choke up on the club, but open the blade of the club by turning the clubface to the right and take a long, gentle swing. The more you fan open the blade, the higher the shot should go because the clubface's loft will be increased. You also will need to aim more to the left to compensate for the open clubface.

The high, soft pitch is similar to the lob shot, but the stance is not as wide and there usually is more green to hit to. Set your hands slightly ahead of the ball and position the ball to the left of the stance. Try to avoid quickly cocking the wrist as you take the club away from the ball. For a soft shot, finish with the hands high.

Preparing for the lob shot

The pitch shot

How to Play the Game

Sand Shots

To explode a ball out of the sand, you will need a sand wedge. This club has a flange that prevents it from digging too far into the sand. Practice as to how much you need to open the clubface. It is usually a different degree according to the consistency of the sand. Many professionals like a wide-open face, but average golfers have to be careful not to hit the ball with the blade of the club. The degree you open the blade also will dictate how far you will hit the ball. The more wide-open the face, the shorter you will hit the ball.

Open your stance and plant your feet firmly in the sand. Your weight should be mostly on the left side and your head ahead of the ball. Swing back with the arms, keeping the body turn to a minimum. On the downswing, pull down with the arms as the weight remains on the left side. Try to hit about 2 inches behind the ball to blast it out of the sand. Follow through naturally.

The sand shot

GOLF

Recovery Shots

When playing golf, you eventually will put the ball in a position that will be difficult to hit or impossible to hit to the green. Do not try a miracle shot or a shot that you have not practiced in these situations. It probably will save you strokes if you are able to chip or pitch the ball back to the fairway and then try to salvage your score.

Also, practice hitting from tall grass by using a sand wedge and repeating the swing you would use out of sand. Just because you are off the green does not mean you have to chip or pitch. If the fringe is cut closely, you might opt to use a putter. When the ball is lodged against the fringe, you can use a 3-wood or blade the ball with the edge of a wedge to roll it toward the hole.

Basically, recovery shots require a lot of practice and imagination.

Pitch From a Bad Lie

Shots from several types of bad lies can be handled with the same technique. The bad lies you might encounter include the ball nestled in a depression, in heavy rough, or in front of a big tuft of grass.

If you have to get the ball up and over a bunker or some other object or hazard, play the shot similar to a sand shot. Use a sand wedge, and open the blade slightly. Aim slightly left to allow for a left-to-right spin on the ball. Pick up the club more quickly than usual with your hands on the backswing, then strike down an inch or two behind the ball.

When going through the impact area, you should feel as if the right hand is sliding the club under the ball. To offset the bounce of the sand wedge and to compensate for hitting behind the ball, you will have to swing harder than you normally would do for the distance. If the shot is too risky, it might be smarter to play to the center of the green rather than at the pin and try to salvage the lowest score possible.

How to Play the Game

Full Shot From Heavy Rough

This is one of the most common shots a golfer will face. Yet, it is the shot that is most often misplayed. Too many players try to whack the ball out of the tall rough with a long iron.

The shot does need to be hit hard, so keep the tension out of the arms and hands to remain loose. If distance is required, use a 5-wood or 7-wood rather than a long iron. Set your weight more to the left and keep the ball positioned normally in your stance. Open the clubface slightly and aim slightly right because the tall grass will wrap itself around the club's hosel, where the shaft or handle is inserted into the clubface, and cause the clubface to close and the ball to be pulled left.

Lift the club a little more quickly than normal on the backswing, which will allow you to come into the ball at a steeper angle. Swing hard and keep the left hand strong throughout the shot. Try to finish high with your hands.

The full shot from heavy rough

Get Out and Play!

Play a round of golf with a parent or with another adult, preferably someone familiar with golf. Play at least one round in a "tournament" against the adult and compete in either match play or stroke play.

Before playing, be sure to mark your golf balls with a unique, identifying mark and review the basic rules. On the course, follow golf etiquette and courtesy. Use a scorecard provided by the course, and have fun!

How to Play the Game

Chart Your Progress

Many golfers maintain a log of their rounds and make notes of which phase of the game they have problems with. By doing this, golfers can chart their progress and know which areas of the game they need to work on during practice.

Date _____ Players _____ Weather _____
Course _____ Rating _____ Slope _____
No. of eagles _____ No. of birdies _____ No. of pars _____ No. of bogies _____

Hole	Yardage	Par	Score	Clubs Used	Putts	Penalties	Fairway Hit	Up and Down	Sand Saves	Green Notes	Other Notes
1											
2											
3											
4											
5											
6											
7											
8											
9											
Front											
10											
11											
12											
13											
14											
15											
16											
17											
18											
Back											
Total											

Safety, First Aid, and Fitness

As with any sport, athletes should be physically and mentally prepared to play golf. It is also important to be prepared for a lengthy period in the outdoors, since a round of golf typically takes three to five hours.

Weather-Related Dangers

When playing, golfers should remain aware of the weather, especially if lightning is in the area or is forecast. Approximately 67 people die each year in the United States because of lightning strikes.

Some golf courses have lightning detectors and will warn players if lightning is getting close. Even if you do not see lightning, it can strike suddenly from gray, low clouds that could be rain clouds. It does not have to be stormy or rainy for lightning to strike. If lightning is a threat, take these precautions:

- Do not hold a golf club.
- Seek shelter inside a building or car, if available, or leave the course immediately. When in a car, avoid touching the metal.
- Do not seek shelter under a tree or under an open shelter, and stay away from water.

If a severe, sudden storm strikes, threatening to harbor a tornado, seek immediate shelter in a ravine, if possible.

Before playing golf, always check the weather forecast. If severe weather is forecast, it might be best to play another day.

> Other possible hazards along the golf course could be fire ants, bees, and wasps. Usually if one does not bother bees or wasps, they will not sting, but fire ants are easily disturbed and swarm quickly. In some areas, snakes and even crocodiles or alligators pose dangers.

SAFETY, FIRST AID, AND FITNESS

Golf Ball Liver—a Golfer's Disease

You may have seen golfers lick the dirt off their golf ball so the ball will roll true or to hold a used tee in their mouth, but can be a dangerous habit. Toxic substances on the courses may cling to the ball and tee. These include fertilizers, pesticides, weed killers, and animal excrement. Some golfers who have a habit of cleaning their golf balls by licking them develop hepatitis, an inflammation of the liver. It is best to always carry a towel in your golf bag and dampen it to wipe your ball clean.

Golf and First Aid

There are a few first-aid issues that apply especially to golfers and golfing.

When we lose more water than we take in, we become dehydrated. Symptoms of mild **dehydration** include increased thirst, dry lips, and dark yellow urine. Symptoms of moderate to severe dehydration include severe thirst, dry mouth with little saliva, dry skin, weakness, dizziness, confusion, nausea, cramping, loss of appetite, decreased sweating (even with exertion), decreased urine production, and dark brown urine. For mild dehydration, drink a quart or two of water or sports drink over two to four hours. Rest for 24 hours and continue drinking fluids. See a physician for moderate to severe dehydration, which requires emergency care.

Heat exhaustion can be brought on by a combination of dehydration and a warm environment. Symptoms include a severe lack of energy, general weakness, headache, nausea, faintness, and sweating; cool, pale, moist skin; and a rapid pulse. If you or anyone in your group shows signs of heat exhaustion, get to a shady, cool spot. Have the person drink small amounts cool water or a sports drink. Apply water to the skin and clothing and fan the person. Raising the legs may help prevent a feeling of faintness. The person should feel better after two or three hours but should rest for the remainder of the day and be extra careful about staying hydrated.

In **heatstroke,** the body's cooling system begins to fail and the person's core temperature rises to life-threatening levels. Dehydration and overexertion, especially in high heat and humidity, can lead to heatstroke. Symptoms can include those of heat exhaustion as well as hot, sweaty, red skin, confusion, disorientation, and a rapid pulse. If you suspect heatstroke in someone, call for medical assistance immediately. Then quickly

Besides injuries, golfers should be aware of other factors when playing, such as the plants that grow on golf courses. Learn what poison oak and poison ivy look like and avoid them.

GOLF 53

Safety, First Aid, and Fitness

work to lower the person's temperature. Move the person to a shady, cool area, loosen tight clothing, and fan the person. Apply wet towels. If you have ice packs, wrap them in a thin barrier (such as a shirt) and place them under the armpits and against the neck and groin. If the person is able to drink, give small amounts of cool water.

> It is best to prevent sunburn. Whenever you are outdoors, use plenty of sunscreen with a sun protection factor (SPF) rating of at least 15. Apply sunscreen liberally about a half-hour before sunlight exposure and reapply every two hours, especially if you are sweating. A broad-brimmed hat, long-sleeved shirt, and long pants provide even more protection. To treat painful sunburn, apply cool, damp, or wet cloths; change the cloths frequently. Stay under shade.

If possible, carry a cell phone on the golf course; in the event of an emergency you may need to contact the pro shop or call 911. However, as a courtesy to others, turn off your cell phone while you are playing.

Blisters. Blisters are pockets of fluid that form when the skin is aggravated by friction. A hot spot—the tender area as a blister starts to form—is a signal to stop immediately. The protection a golf glove gives you should help prevent blisters on the hand. However, to help prevent foot blisters, wear golf shoes that fit and pay attention to how your feet feel. To treat a hot spot, cover the tender area with a piece of moleskin or molefoam slightly larger than the hot spot. Use several layers if necessary. If you must drain a blister, clean the area first. Then sterilize a pin in the flame of a match, prick the blister near its lower edge, and press out the fluid. Change bandages every day to help keep wounds clean and avoid infection. Diabetics who develop blisters should see a physician.

Sprains and Strains. A *sprain* occurs when a joint is bent far enough to overstretch the ligaments, the tough bands that hold joints together. Twisting an ankle is one way a person could sustain a sprain. A *strain* occurs when muscles are over-stretched, creating tears in the muscle fibers, such as lower back pain from muscles strained by overuse or by lifting loads that are too heavy.

To treat sprains and strains, have the victim take any weight off of the injured joint and instruct the person not to use the joint. Do not try to move or straighten an injured limb. Apply ice packs or cold compresses to the limb for no more than 20 minutes at a time. Be sure to place a barrier such as a thin towel between the ice pack and bare skin. Seek medical treatment if the pain persists or is severe.

Physical and Mental Fitness

Golf can be beneficial physically—especially if one walks while playing—as well as mentally.

Overall fitness will help prevent injuries. Golfers should develop their cardiovascular system by jogging, walking, climbing stairs, or cycling. Jogging is a good way to become fit because all it requires is a good pair of running shoes. Try to work upward so that you can jog at least 30 minutes at a time, three times a week.

Because golfers once believed that some exercises, such as weight training, would impede their swings, they did little to strengthen their bodies. More modern players, however, have discovered that being fit can help to prevent injuries and improve their stamina throughout tournaments. In some high schools and colleges, coaches are requiring their players to at least jog to improve their fitness levels.

> If you are not accustomed to exercising, work into the activities slowly to avoid injuries.

> Golf is considered by many to be a sport that poses little chance of injury and that does not require a high level of physical activity. However, there is plenty of physical movement in a swing and potential for injuries to the back, elbows, knees, hips, or wrists—especially to players who are not physically fit.

You also can improve mentally because golf requires competitors to learn how to handle pressure and control emotions, eliminate or control negative thoughts, and think positively, visualize a shot, and trust themselves and their abilities.

Because success in golf can be as much mental as physical, some sports psychologists specialize in helping golfers. Some golfers visit a sports psychologist for a mental tune-up as well as an instructor for a swing tune-up.

Exercises

Before exercise and physical fitness became popular among professional golfers, the 5-foot-7-inch, 150-pound Gary Player already had endorsed a healthy lifestyle that included exercise and eating properly. That Player continued to play well and healthy into his 60s should be a testament to how a healthy lifestyle can benefit not only a golfer, but anyone.

Player believes "physical fitness is the key to top performance and success . . . on the golf course, behind a desk, in the classroom, or in the kitchen." His exercise regimen has

Safety, First Aid, and Fitness

When Tiger Woods won so many major tournaments in his early 20s, other pros noticed how fit he was. Many stepped up their own workout routines to improve their conditioning. Pros Vijay Singh, and Ernie Els both saw measurable improvement in their golf game after boosting their fitness routine.

included skipping rope, knee bends, running, fingertip push-ups, squeezing a small sponge rubber ball, swinging weighted clubs, pulling himself up a rope, and working hard around his ranch in South Africa. He does warn against bulking up by using heavy weights because he believes large muscles can ruin a golf swing.

Player has complemented his exercising by following a diet that includes plenty of whole grains, fish, vegetables, fruits, and meat. He avoids fried foods, sugar, potatoes, white bread, rich desserts, coffee, tea, and alcohol. He also abhors smoking.

It was not long before other players on the PGA Tour began realizing that to compete for very long at a high level, they also needed to be fit. Regardless of their fitness level, golfers are susceptible to injury to certain parts of the body, such as the elbow, hip, knee, and lower back. To strengthen those areas, golfers should exercise.

Player has several exercise suggestions.

For the hands and wrists: Tightly squeeze a rubber ball or a hand-squeezing spring device. Clench it for seven seconds, release, and squeeze again. Repeat this several times with both hands. Do this as often as possible during the day.

For the legs: If you have weights, you can do half-squats and toe raises with the weights across your shoulders. If you do not have weights, running is the best way to strengthen the legs. It improves leg stamina and the cardiovascular system. Player also recommends jogging and kangaroo jumps—standing on your toes, squatting down, and springing as high as possible into the air. Do this 10 to 15 times, twice a day.

Another good leg exercise is the wall sit. Simulate a sitting position with your back flat against a wall, your arms dangling at your sides, and your feet spread widely apart. Hold this position for a minute at first, but build up to two minutes. Repeat several times.

The wal

A one-legged squat also is one of Player's favorites. Put one leg and your arms out from your body while standing. Then do a knee bend on the other leg.

For the forearms and wrists: Hold a dumbbell in each hand with a weight that you can hold at arm's length and shoulder height. Twirl the wrists clockwise for 10 seconds and then counterclockwise for 10 seconds. Bring your arms to your sides and do the same thing. If you do not have dumbbells, just put your arms out and double the amount of time you twirl your wrists.

The one-legged squat

56   GOLF

= SAFETY, FIRST AID, AND FITNESS

The American Academy of Orthopaedic Surgeons suggests similar exercises to strengthen the forearms. Take a lightweight dumbbell and lower the weight to the end of your fingers. Then curl the weight back into your palm, followed by curling your wrist to lift the weight an inch or two higher. Do 10 repetitions with each arm.

You also can do reverse wrist curls by using the same lightweight dumbbell. Place your hands in front of you, palms down. Using your wrist, lift the weight up and down. Hold the arm you are exercising above your elbow with your other hand to limit the motion to your forearm. Do 10 repetitions with each arm.

Lower Back Pain

The rotational stresses of the golf swing place considerable pressure on the spine and muscles, and can cause lower back pain. Poor flexibility and muscle strength can make one more prone to this injury. Also, golfers with bad swing techniques are more prone to hurt their backs.

One of the best ways for golfers to avoid back problems is to do some simple stretching exercises before playing a round of golf and then warm up by hitting some golf balls. Start out with a short club, such as a pitching wedge or 9-iron, and work up to the longer clubs, such as the 2-iron and 3-iron. Do not start out taking full swings, but rather begin by hitting short pitch shots with a half-swing.

Here are some exercises to help strengthen lower back muscles.

With the rubber tubing still tied, kneel and hold the tubing over your head. Pull down slowly toward your chest, bending your elbows as you lower your arms. Raise the tubing slowly over your head. Do three sets of 10 repetitions at least three times a week.

Firmly tie together the ends of rubber tubing and place the loop around an object that is shoulder height. Standing with your arms straight out in front, grasp the tubing and slowly pull it toward your chest. Release slowly. Do three sets of 10 repetitions at least three times a week.

GOLF 57

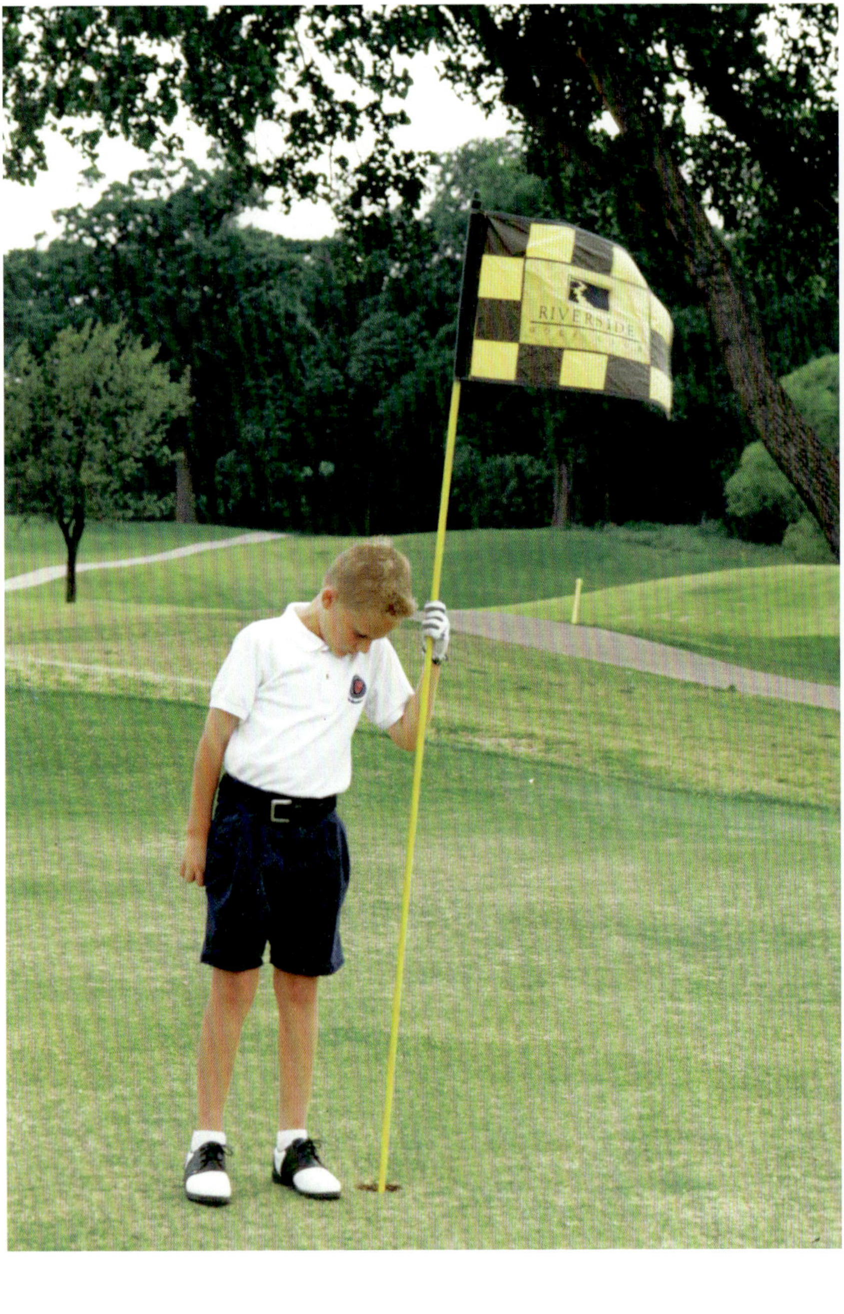
RIVERSIDE

Conduct and Procedures on the Golf Course

Besides following the "Rules of Golf," players should also follow a code of decent and friendly conduct. This code includes safety, courtesy, fast play, and care of the course.

Courtesy and Fast Play

- When it is someone else's turn to play, do not move, talk, or stand too close or in his line of vision.
- Play at an appropriate pace; do not dally. Be prepared to hit when it is your turn. Line up your shot while others are lining up theirs. Leave the green as soon as all players in your group have finished the hole. Slow play has become a major problem at golf courses.
- Let faster players play through.
- When on the greens, do not step in the line of another player's putt.
- Play usually is in turn, with the player farthest from the hole hitting first, but in informal play, it is often prudent to hit when ready to help speed play.
- When replacing the flagstick, do so carefully to avoid damaging the hole.

CONDUCT AND PROCEDURES ON THE GOLF COURSE

Care of the Course

Be respectful of the golf course wherever you play. Dispose of trash in the trash receptacles on the course, or pack it out in your golf bag. If you are using a cart, stay on the cart path and along designated routes.

- After hitting from a bunker, be sure to rake where you walked and the area from where you hit. Do not leave the rake lying in the sand.

- Replace all divots—turf that is ripped up after a shot (usually with an iron).

- Use a divot tool to repair your ball mark or others' ball marks after hitting to a green. This not only keeps the surface smooth for upcoming players but also helps the grass heal. Repair any spike marks (many courses do not allow metal spikes) and walk carefully on greens. Do not drag your feet.

- Avoid unnecessary practice swings to avoid damaging turf during the swing.

Basically, try to leave the course in the condition you would like to find it.

Marking your ball

Replacing a divot

The Rules of Golf

Golf, as all sports, has rules that must be followed. The Royal and Ancient Golf Club of St. Andrews and the United States Golf Association write and interpret the rules. Any rules changes occur every four years when the two groups meet to discuss possible changes. While there are too many rules to list here, you should learn some basic procedures and rules before playing.

- It may help to pen a unique identifying mark on your golf balls to distinguish them from those of the other players.

- Arrive at the first tee on time for your scheduled start.

- Announce your handicap to other players if it is a handicap tournament.

- Play with undue delay. Be ready to hit when it is your turn.

- Play the ball as it lies unless local rules permit you to touch or move the ball.

Conduct and Procedures on the Golf Course

- Play the course as you find it. Do not improve the lie of the ball or the area of the intended swing or line of play.
- If you are in a hazard, do not ground (touch the ground or water with your club) before striking the ball or you will incur a penalty.
- You are allowed up to 14 clubs (any mix) in your golf bag during a round.
- You cannot ask or get advice from anyone other than your caddie or partner, if playing on a team.
- Do not play the wrong ball; that is why you mark it. In match play, you would lose the hole. In stroke play, you would incur a two-stroke penalty and possible disqualification.

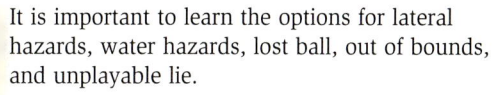

It is important to learn the options for lateral hazards, water hazards, lost ball, out of bounds, and unplayable lie.

- Lateral hazards should be defined by red stakes or lines. If you hit into a lateral hazard, here are your options:

   1. Play the ball as it lies without penalty.
   2. Drop a ball behind the hazard, keeping the point at which the original ball last crossed the margin of the hazard directly between the hole and the spot on which the ball is dropped, with no limit to how far behind the hazard the ball may be dropped, and taking a one-stroke penalty.
   3. Follow stroke-and-distance procedure and hit from the original spot with a one-stroke penalty.

GOLF 61

Conduct and Procedures on the Golf Course

   4. Drop within two club lengths of the point where the ball entered the hazard and no closer to the hole, and take a one-stroke penalty.
   5. Drop a ball outside the hazard within two club lengths of and not nearer the hole than a point on the opposite margin of the hazard that is an equal distance from the hole.
- A water hazard, excluding lateral, should be defined by yellow stakes or lines. If you hit into a water hazard, these are your options:
   1. Hit the ball as it lies without penalty.
   2. Follow stroke-and-distance procedure by hitting from the original spot with a one-stroke penalty.
   3. Drop a ball behind the water hazard, keeping the point at which the original ball last crossed the margin of the water hazard directly between the hole and the spot on which the ball is dropped, with no limit to how far behind the water hazard the ball may be dropped, and taking a one-stroke penalty.
- If a ball is lost or is out of bounds, you should play a ball, under penalty of one stroke, as close as possible to the spot from where the original ball was last played.
- A player may declare the ball unplayable at any place on the course except when the ball is in a water hazard. If the ball is deemed unplayable, you may do any one of the following:
   1. Play a ball, under penalty of one stroke, as near as possible to the spot where the original ball was played.
   2. Drop a ball, within two club lengths from the spot where the original ball laid, but not closer to the hole.
   3. Drop a ball, behind the point where the ball lay, keeping that point directly between the hole and the spot on which the ball is dropped, with no limit to how far behind that point the ball may be dropped.
- When a ball is hit out of bounds, usually outside an area marked by white stakes or lines, play a ball from as close as possible to the original spot, under penalty of one stroke.
- If you breach the rules during match or stroke play and must incur a penalty, you must tell your opponent so that he or she knows the status of the match. If, during match play, you

===== Conduct and Procedures on the Golf Course

believe your opponent has broken a rule, make your claim before teeing off on the next hole. If you wait until playing the next hole, it will be too late.
- If you are playing stroke play, carefully check your score on each hole after your round. If you sign a card with a lower score on a hole than you actually made, penalty is disqualification. If you sign for a higher score on a hole, the score will stand.

You should carry a small rules book in your golf bag. *If you are in a tournament and do not understand a rule, ask an official for an interpretation.*

Rules of Amateur Status

Amateur golf is for fun and sport. Often, business deals and connections have been made on the golf course. Certainly, many friendships have been made.

Throughout most of golf's history, there has been a distinct difference between amateurs and professionals. The purpose for this is to provide a basis for fair competition because the professional should hold an advantage over the amateur in playing skill. The USGA has a long list of rules that a player must follow to protect his amateur status. The most common violations of those rules are:

- Playing for prize money.
- Receiving payment for teaching golf.
- Accepting a tournament prize that exceeds $500 retail value, except a symbolic prize such as a trophy that is intended for display.
- Accepting golf equipment from a dealer without proper payment.
- Accepting certain expenses to play in golf tournaments. There are some exceptions, including for junior competitions and when representing one's school or college.

Harry Vardon

Major Influences

Hundreds, if not thousands, of officials, players, developers, and managers have influenced the game of golf. Among those who are most significant are Joseph C. Dey, former executive director of the USGA and first commissioner of the Tournament Players Division, and Deane Bernan, who succeeded Dey and directed the PGA Tour into a rich, viable, nationwide tour. The list of influences includes former players such as Paul Runyan, Gene Sarazen, Bobby Locke, Sam Snead, Charlie Sifford, Lee Elder, Althea Gibson, Seve Ballesteros, and Tom Watson, as well as course architects such as Pete Dye and sports agents such as Mark McCormack. Each has influenced the game, most notably increasing the game's popularity.

Harry Vardon and Bobby Jones

Englishman Harry Vardon and American Bobby Jones were two early golfers whose precision play and success made them heroes in their own countries. It was said of Vardon, who played in the late 1800s and early 1900s, that if he played a course twice, he was so accurate that he would play out of his same divots the second time around. Because he had big hands, the right-handed Vardon devised an overlapping grip, which still bears his name.

Jones pulled off golf's most famous feat in 1930 when he won the grand slam of that time—the British and U.S. Opens and the British and U.S. Amateurs. No one else has won four major tournaments in the same year. Jones retired from competitive golf later that year at the ripe old age of 28. Jones' record includes winning the British Open three times, the U.S. Open four times, the British Amateur once, and the U.S. Amateur four times.

Bobby Jones

MAJOR INFLUENCES

Ben Hogan and Byron Nelson

These two Texans caddied together and learned how to play at Glen Garden Golf and Country Club in Fort Worth, Texas.

Hogan, known for spending hours on the practice tee to hone his swing, is considered one of golf's greatest. He won 63 PGA Tour titles and was the leading money winner among American professionals from 1940 to 1942 and in 1946 and 1948. He captured the hearts of many when he rebounded from severe injuries suffered in a bus collision in 1949. Only 17 months later, Hogan came back to win his second of four U.S. Open titles while limping around on wrapped legs. His comeback inspired a 1951 movie, *Follow the Sun.* Hogan won two PGA Championship titles, two Masters, and one British Open, which gave him a career gland slam.

Byron Nelson is recognized by many as the first to adopt a "modern" swing after switching from wooden shafts to steel shafts. He won an unprecedented 11 consecutive tournaments in 1945 and won 18 tournaments that year, while averaging 68.3 strokes a round. His swing was so consistent that a golf-swinging machine to test golf balls and clubs was dubbed "Iron Byron."

Nelson, who won money in 113 consecutive tournaments, including two Masters, a U.S. Open, and two PGA Championships, retired from playing full-time early in his career, in 1946. He later worked as a television golf analyst and became the first and only golfer to have a tournament named after him, the Byron Nelson Classic. He also is known for his untiring work for charities and other golf-related causes.

The Big Three

Jack Nicklaus, Arnold Palmer, and Gary Player each had his own illustrious career, and because the three dominated professional golf much of the 1960s and '70s, they became known as the Big Three. A tournament's prestige often was measured on whether at least one of the Big Three competed. They also became friendly rivals, and a television series of "Big Three Golf" was produced that featured the three playing against each other.

Arnold Palmer's charisma and his ability to fashion comebacks during the dawn of television golf coverage in the late 1950s and early '60s made him one of the game's most revered players. He had a throng of fans, appropriately dubbed "Arnie's Army."

MAJOR INFLUENCES

One of his biggest achievements and what gave him his reputation for comebacks were the Masters and U.S. Open in 1960. At the Masters, Palmer birdied the final two holes of the tournament to edge Ken Venturi by one stroke. In the Open, which was a 36-hole finish back then, Palmer came from seven shots behind to finish the final round with a 65. In typical Palmer fashion, he ignored the trouble on the first short par-4 hole and drove the green to begin his rally.

Throughout his career, Palmer won four Masters (1958, 1960, 1962, and 1964), the 1960 U.S. Open, and the 1961 and 1962 British Open titles.

Jack Nicklaus

Arnold Palmer

Gary Player

GOLF 67

Major Influences

When Jack Nicklaus turned professional in 1962, he immediately showed that he would be Palmer's main rival by winning the U.S. Open that year. He often bested the popular Palmer and so was not well-liked at first by many golf enthusiasts. He eventually won them over with his outstanding play and a physical makeover that included growing out his short, blond hair and trimming his weight. This resulted in his nickname, the Golden Bear.

Nicklaus has won an unprecedented 18 major titles. He won six Masters (1963, 1965, 1966, 1972, 1975, and 1986, when he became the oldest Masters winner at age 46); five PGA Championships (1963, 1971, 1973, 1975, 1980), four U.S. Open titles (1962, 1967, 1972, 1980), and three British Open championships (1966, 1970, 1978).

Also during that time, South African Gary Player began exerting himself. Player won three Masters (1961, 1974, and 1978), two PGA titles (1962 and 1972), three British Opens (1959, 1968, and 1974), and one U.S. Open (1965). He became only the third golfer after Gene Sarazen and Ben Hogan to win a career grand slam by winning all four major tournaments.

Because of their prolific wins and dominance of the game of golf during this period, Palmer, Nicklaus, and Player became three of the biggest names in golf.

Lee Trevino

When he became a major force on the PGA Tour, Lee Trevino proved that you do not have to grow up at country clubs and have a picture-perfect swing to be successful at golf. He grew up poor and developed an unorthodox swing that includes an open stance, a closed clubface, and a blocking-out move on the downswing that promoted a fade.

Trevino's family lived close to a golf course, and he honed his game by working at a driving range in Dallas, Texas. He also caddied and worked as a greenkeeper. He played his golf at municipal courses and often would play against opponents using only one club, or using a soft drink bottle wrapped in tape as a club. He joined the PGA Tour in 1966 after a stint in the Marines and won the U.S. Open just two years later.

Lee Trevino

Trevino has said his biggest moment came when he beat Jack Nicklaus in an 18-hole playoff to win the 1971 U.S. Open. He caused some ripples when he refused to play the Masters for several years. While he said it was because the course did not suit his game, some speculated that he also was protesting the Augusta National Golf Club's past racial policies. He would change his shoes in his car and seldom enter the clubhouse when he did play there. During his career, Trevino won two U.S. Open titles, two British Open titles, and three PGA Championships.

Tiger Woods

Possibly no one has made a bigger impact on golf's popularity among golfers and nongolfers than Eldrick "Tiger" Woods. Tiger's unusual nickname was given to him by his father, Earl Woods, after a Vietnamese soldier who was his friend. Earl started his youngster swinging a golf club as soon as Tiger could walk. It was not long before Tiger became a golf prodigy. When he was only 2 years old, Tiger putted against comedian Bob Hope on the "Mike Douglas Show." At age 3, Tiger shot a 48 for nine holes. He was featured in a *Golf Digest* story at age 5.

By the time Tiger turned 6, he had recorded two holes in one. At 15, he became the youngest player to win the U.S. Junior National Championship and already was amazing followers of golf with his distance off the tee and overall play. By the time he had won his third U.S. Amateur—the only golfer to win three consecutive U.S. Amateur titles—he was showing his potential to dominate the game at any level.

Woods turned professional in 1996; the next year, at age 21, he became the youngest to win the Masters. Woods was also the first African American and first Asian American to win the Masters. When he won the 1997 Masters, he set several records, including the lowest score for 72 holes (18-under-par 270) and the widest margin of victory (12 strokes).

Tiger Woods

Major Influences

In 2000, Woods won the U.S. Open, the PGA Championship, and the British Open in dominating fashion, and he won a fourth consecutive major tournament the next year at the Masters. But because the four victories were not in the same year, the outstanding feat—though grand—was not considered a traditional grand slam. In 2007, when Tiger Woods was 31 years old, he won his 13th major title, putting him ahead of the pace Jack Nicklaus set for his own major title record. Nicklaus was 35 when he won his 13th career major title. Woods' major titles include four Masters, two U.S. Open, three British Open, and four PGA Championship wins. In the same year, he won his seventh PGA Grand Slam.

His success has sparked unprecedented interest among minorities and youths. The National Golf Foundation reports that junior golf's participation grew 34 percent, to 2.4 million, in 1997 when Woods began making his big impact. His presence continues to drive more interest in golf.

To help those who cannot afford to play, the Tiger Woods Foundation was formed in 1996 by Tiger and his father, Earl. The Tiger Woods Foundation has pledged its full support of the First Tee program, formed by the World Golf Foundation and PGA Tour in 1997. The First Tee program helps fund programs for underprivileged youth and individuals with disabilities, golf occupational programs for economically disadvantaged youth, and alternative facilities development for accessibility to people with disabilities.

Influential Women Golfers

While men have dominated golf throughout most of history, women now account for about 40 percent of new golfers. However, they make up only about 13 percent of the total number of players.

Probably the first woman to generate wide public interest in golf was Mildred "Babe" Didrikson-Zaharias, a multitalented athlete. She excelled in basketball and won two gold medals and a silver in the high jump, high hurdles, and javelin in the 1932 Olympics in Los Angeles. Then she took up golf, and through hours and months of grueling practice, she became the top woman

Babe Didrikson-Zaharias

MAJOR INFLUENCES

player. She won every major amateur golf tournament in the next 15 years and helped form the Ladies Professional Golf Association in 1950.

Before she died of cancer in 1956, Didrikson-Zaharias had won 55 amateur and professional tournaments, including five majors. Her power off the tee allowed her to hit farther than many men; she virtually overpowered golf courses.

Another strong player, Mickey Wright, possessed a near-perfect swing. Ben Hogan and Byron Nelson said she had the best swing they had seen. Before her career ended, Wright won 82 professional tournaments. She was such an attraction that sponsors would threaten to cancel their tournaments if she did not play. She joined the tour in 1955 and won her first professional tournament in 1956. Among her victories were four U.S. Women's Open titles and four LPGA Championships. She won 13 titles in 1963.

If there are any parallels in women's golf to men's golf and Tiger Woods, it probably would be Nancy Lopez. She had a hugely successful amateur career and left college early to turn professional in 1977. She was an immediate hit. She finished second in her first three tournaments, and her charisma and personality won over her peers, the gallery, and the media. Whenever she played, television coverage often followed her.

Lopez has a powerful, though unorthodox, swing and, despite her relaxed attitude, she is an intense competitor. She had 35 tour victories by the time she was 30. In 1978, she won nine tournaments, including her first of three LPGA Championships. Heading into 2002, Lopez had won 48 titles, including three LPGA titles.

Nancy Lopez

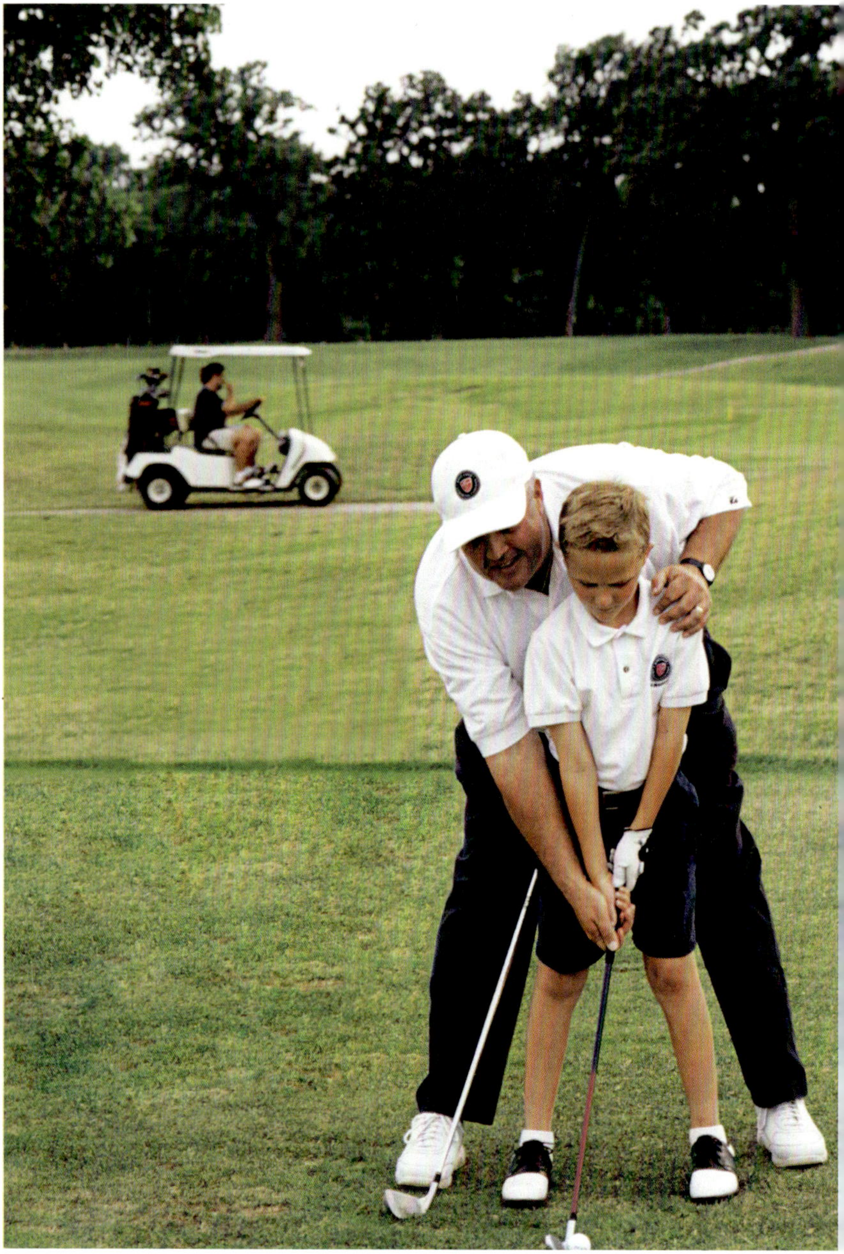

Careers in Golf

Because of the many facets of golf, there are a variety of careers available even if one is not a great player. First, there is a need for architects to design and build courses. Then there are those who work at various jobs at the clubhouses and pro shops. Courses need maintenance personnel, and the PGA of America has sectional offices throughout the country that need personnel. These sectional sites usually are clearinghouses for positions in their particular area, and one of their functions is to conduct tournaments for their sectional professionals. Here are some of the typical positions associated with golf.

Club Professional

Most golf professionals serve at public and private golf courses, where they provide lessons, operate golf shops, direct a staff, and help conduct tournaments. A club professional must attend schools conducted by the PGA, pass playing tests, and complete an apprentice program. In 1994, the PGA began its Golf Professional Training program, which replaced previous programs.

Although club professionals are tied to a club, they often have tournaments that pit them against their peers.

Touring Professionals

While club professionals sometimes compete in tournaments, other players devote themselves to tournament play and make their living by competing for prize money. They often travel nationwide and worldwide to compete.

The PGA Tour and the LPGA Tour are the two organizations in the United States that offer the most prize money for men and women professionals. There also are tours worldwide. Satellite tours are available for players who are hoping to elevate their games and earn playing privileges on the larger tours. There also are tours for senior players, such as the Senior PGA Tour.

Professional Instructors

Although club professionals offer lessons among their other duties, some professionals concentrate only on teaching. Many teach at instructional centers and use technology that includes video to show different angles of swings and that can allow comparisons of students' swings with those of the great players. Some instructors specialize in certain areas of the game, such as the short game. Many of the world's top players usually have an instructor who constantly monitors their game.

Sports Psychologist

Because golf can be as much a mental challenge as a physical challenge, a growing number of golfers work with sports psychologists. These specially trained professionals work with athletes to help them eliminate negative thoughts and concentrate on positive thoughts, among other things. Many top amateur and professional golfers have sought this type of help.

Golf Course Superintendent

The golf course superintendent coordinates the management and maintenance of the course with the club manager and the golf professional. A superintendent monitors the course's condition and playability and works with a crew to ensure that day-to-day tasks such as mowing, watering, raking bunkers, and repairing divots are done. The golf course superintendent must know the "Rules of Golf," have administrative abilities to manage a budget and staff as well as technical knowledge about turf management, water conservation, drainage, and irrigation systems, appropriate use of insecticides and fungicides, and the protection of ecological systems on the course. Often, a course superintendent has had formal education relating to plant science or landscaping, or has met the requirements to be professionally certified through a program offered by the Golf Course Superintendents Association of America.

Architect

With the growing number of golf courses being built, there has been an increase in the number golf course designers and architects. Designing courses usually involves knowledge of landscaping, engineering, turf, grasses, and environmental statutes. Some well-known playing professionals, including Arnold Palmer and Jack Nicklaus, have entered this profession and will offer their input about course design in partnership with a known architect.

Management

Many courses being built are open to the public, and management companies often are hired to operate the clubs. Many municipalities have leased their courses to management companies. Management companies hire their own employees to operate the clubhouse and to maintain the course.

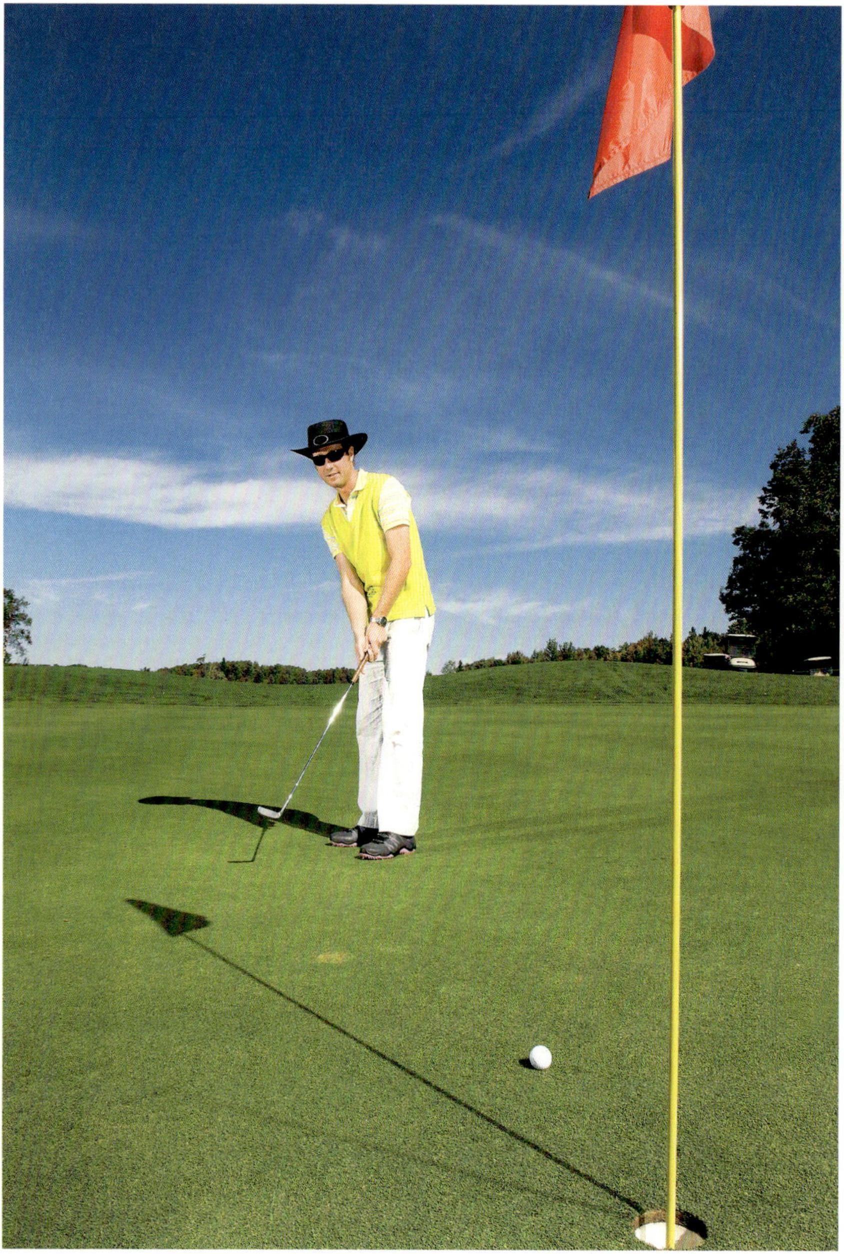

Golf Resources

Scouting Literature

Deck of First Aid; Emergency First Aid pocket guide; *Athletics, First Aid, Personal Fitness,* and *Sports* merit badge pamphlets

> Visit the Boy Scouts of America's official retail Web site at *http://www.scoutstuff.org* for a complete listing of all merit badge pamphlets and other helpful Scouting materials and supplies.

Books

Cook, Kevin. *Tommy's Honor: The Story of Old Tom Morris and Young Tom Morris, Golf's Founding Father and Son.* Penguin Group, 2007.

Davis, Martin, and Ken Venturi, Dan Jenkins, and Tom Watson. *Byron Nelson: The Story of Golf's Greatest Gentleman and the Greatest Winning Streak in History.* The American Golfer, 1997.

Els, Ernie, with David Herman. *Ernie Els' Guide to Golf Fitness: How Staying in Shape Will Take Strokes Off Your Game and Add Yards to Your Drives.* Crown Publishing Group, 2001.

Hogan, Ben, and Herbert Warren Wind. *Ben Hogan's Five Lessons: The Modern Fundamentals of Golf.* Pocket Books, 1990.

Jones, Robert Trent. *Golf by Design: How to Lower Your Score by Reading the Features of a Course.* Little, Brown and Company, 2005.

Leadbetter, David. *The Golf Swing.* Penguin Group, 2001.

Nicklaus, Jack, with Ken Bowden. *Golf My Way.* Simon & Schuster Adult Publishing Group, 2005.

Peary, Danny, and Allen F. Richardson, eds. *Great Golf: 150 Years of Essential Instruction.* Stewart, Tabori & Chang, 2005.

Pelz, Dave, with James A. Frank. *Dave Pelz's Putting Bible: The Complete Guide to Mastering the Green.* Doubleday Publishing, 2000.

———. *Dave Pelz's Short Game Bible: Master the Finesse Swing and Lower Your Score.* Random House, 1999.

Penick, Harvey, with Bud Shrake. *Harvey Penick's Little Red Book: Lessons and Teachings from a Lifetime in Golf.* Simon & Schuster, 1999.

Golf Resources

Rotella, Dr. Bob, with Bob Cullen. *Golf is a Game of Confidence.* Simon & Schuster Adult Publishing Group, 1996.

Russell, Mark, and John Andrisani. *Golf Rules Plain & Simple.* HarperCollins, 1999.

Shackelford, Geoff. *Grounds for Golf: The History and Fundamentals of Golf Course Design.* Thomas Dunne Books, 2003.

St. Pierre, Denise. *Golf Fundamentals: A Better Way to Learn the Basics.* Human Kinetics Publishers, 2004.

Tait, Alistair. *Golf: The Legends of the Game.* Firefly Books, 2003.

United States Golf Association. *The Rules of Golf.* United States Golf Association, 2007.

Utley, Stan, with Matthew Rudy. *The Art of Putting: The Revolutionary Feel-Based System for Improving Your Score.* Penguin Group, 2006.

Venturi, Ken, with Don Wade. *Ken Venturi's Stroke Savers.* NTC Publishing Group, 1995.

Woods, Tiger. *How I Play Golf.* Little, Brown Book Group, 2004.

Periodicals

Golf Digest and *Golf World*
P.O. Box 850
Wilton, CT 06897

Golf Magazine
P.O. Box 60001
Tampa, FL 33660

Golfweek
The Golfweek Group
1500 Park Center Drive
Orlando, FL 32835-5705

Organizations and Web Sites

American Junior Golf Association
1980 Sports Club Drive
Braselton, GA 30517
Web site: *http://www.ajga.org*

The First Tee
Web site: *http://www.thefirsttee.org*

Junior Golf Showcase
1225 West Main, Suite 110
Norman, OK 73069
Web site: *http://www.juniorgolfshowcase.com*

PING American College Golf Guide
Web site: *http://www.collegegolf.com*

Professional Golfers' Association of America
Web site: *http://www.pga.com*

Professional Golfers' Association Tour
Web site: *http://www.pgatour.com*

U.S. Golf Association
Web site: *http://www.usga.org*

U.S. Kids Golf
3040 Northwoods Parkway
Norcross, GA 30071
Web site: *http://www.uskidsgolf.com*

U.S. Sports Camps
750 Lindaro St., Suite 220
San Rafael, CA 94901
Web site: *http://www.ussportscamps.com*

Acknowledgments

Thanks to the writer, Charles Clines, for bringing the merit badge pamphlet up-to-date and making it functional and fun for Scouts. Mr. Clines is a retired golf columnist for the *Fort Worth Star-Telegram* and is a former golf professional.

The Boy Scouts of America thanks Tracey Stewart for the use of a family photo of Payne Stewart.

The BSA is grateful to the United States Golf Association for its assistance in the early stages of this new edition. USGA experts included Rhonda Glenn, manager of communications; Genger Fahleson, manager of rules education; Kevin O'Connor, senior director; and Peter Dennis, assistant director of handicapping and course rating.

Thanks also go to Johnny Cake, director of golf at Finley Golf Course, University of North Carolina at Chapel Hill, for his help.

We appreciate the Quicklist Consulting Committee of the Association for Library Service to Children, a division of the American Library Association, for its assistance with updating the resources section of this merit badge pamphlet.

Photo and Illustration Credits

©Jupiterimages.com—pages 8, 22, 40, and 75–76 *(both)*

©2005 Jupiterimages Corp.—cover *(tees, ball on tee)*

Ladies Professional Golf Association, courtesy—page 70

PGA TOUR Photographic Services, courtesy—pages 67–69 *(all)*

©Photos.com—cover *(all except merit badge, tees, and ball on tee)*

Bill Steber, courtesy—page 71

Tracey Stewart, courtesy—page 14 *(right)*

U.S. Golf Association, courtesy—pages 10, 13 *(top)*, 14 *(left)*, and 64–65 *(both)*

All other photos and illustrations are the property of or are protected by the Boy Scouts of America.

Dan Bryant—pages 13 *(bottom)*, 46–50 *(all)*, 56–61 *(all)*, 72, and 74

John McDearmon—all illustrations on pages 30–31 and 37

Randy Piland—pages 4 and 39

Notes